GLASNEVIN

GLASNEVIN

MAURICE CURTIS

The History Press Ireland

First published 2014

The History Press Ireland
50 City Quay
Dublin 2
Ireland
www.thehistorypress.ie

British Library Cataloguing in Publication Data.
A catalogue record for this book is available from the British Library.

ISBN 978 1 84588 850 3

Typesetting and origination by The History Press

CONTENTS

ACKNOWLEDGEMENTS

The Glasnevin Heritage network does enormous work to promote interest in this fascinating area and for this I am very grateful. My thanks also goes to Dara McCarthy for his information on Glasnevin North/Ballymun Avenue and to Ann O'Hanlon of St Columba's Road for her invaluable help on the history of the parish of Iona Road. To Fr Richard Sheehy and parishioners of Our Lady of Dolours' church, many thanks. I am very grateful to the former parish priest of St Columba's church, Fr Jim Caffrey, to Teresa Murphy and the Centenary Committee of St Columba's, all of whom did Trojan work for the centenary celebrations in 2005 and I am very thankful for their invaluable assistance. Betty O'Brien is a veritable walking encyclopaedia of Glasnevin and St Columba's parish life and is indeed a mine of information on so many aspects of the area. The Glasnevin Musical Society, the Glasnevin Trust, the Glasnevin Cemeteries Committee, Angela Quinn and staff of the National Botanic Gardens/OPW and Met Éireann, and Na Fianna GAA Club were all very helpful. The late Shane MacThomais, that inspiring guide and historian of Glasnevin Cemetery, deserves a particular mention. Teresa Whitington of the CCL opened the archive on Glasnevin and St Columba's Parish and the wider area. The staff of Pearse Street Public Library were particularly helpful, and likewise the Gilbert Library. The National Library of Ireland, the National Archives, the Irish Architectural Archive, Dublin.ie Forums, the RSAI, the Irish Photographic Archive, and MC's Fotofinish were a great source of information. Colm Graham in his reminiscences and Brendan Scally in his sketches both capture the essence of Glasnevin. June O'Reilly of the Business Depot continues to perform miracles. Thanks also to Ronan Colgan and Beth Amphlett of the History Press for their encouragement and skills. Finally, a hearty thanks to the residents of Glasnevin who were particularly kind, encouraging and helpful in so many ways.

INTRODUCTION

Glasnevin is a mainly residential neighbourhood, located on the north side of the city of Dublin (about 3km north of Dublin City centre) and originally established on the northern bank of the River Tolka. It is bordered to the north by Finglas, to the north-east by Ballymun, to the east by Whitehall, to the south by Phibsboro and Drumcondra, and to the west by Cabra. Glasnevin is part of the Dáil Éireann constituency of Dublin Central. There are many famous people associated with Glasnevin, including legendary football commentator Micheal O'Hehir, U2 frontman Bono, Dublin footballer Robbie Kelleher, writers Jonathan Swift and Richard Brinsley Sheridan, St Mobhi, St Canice and St Columba, and many more.

There is no place in Dublin like Glasnevin. The area has a unique charm, with its old-world gardens, redbrick Alexander Strain homes and a vibrant community of young families, their senior counterparts and university students.

The name Glasnevin, like most Dublin suburbs' titles, comes from Irish Gaelic. It either comes from *Glas Naíon*, meaning 'stream of the infants' or *Glas Naedhe*, meaning 'stream of O'Naeidhe' after an ancient chieftain who established ownership of the area some time before the arrival of the Anglo-Normans.

Glasnevin was established as an area of note by St Mobhi, who founded a monastery and monastic school in the village in the sixth century. St Mobhi's church is still in Glasnevin village, although it became Anglican in the Reformation. The small lane on which it sits was also the location of the home of Jonathan Swift. The monastery continued to be used for many years. St Colman is recorded as having paid homage to its founder when he returned from abroad a century after St Mobhi's death in 544. Mobhi is believed to have been the man who trained St Columba of Iona fame and Glasnevin's longest road, Iona Road, is named in his honour.

Jonathan Swift (1667–1745), author of *Gulliver's Travels*. He was Dean of St Patrick's Cathedral Dublin (1715–1745). (Courtesy of St Patrick's Cathedral)

After the coming of the Normans, the lands of Glasnevin were granted to the Priory of the Holy Trinity attached to Christ Church, and a manorial village replaced the older settlement.

Glasnevin went on to witness some of the pivotal changes in Irish society, including the Battle of Clontarf in 1014, when Brian Boru's soldiers encamped in Glasnevin, along the banks of the River Tolka.

The nature of Glasnevin's development was influenced by its proximity to Dublin City and a move from a largely agricultural village to a more urban suburb gained momentum as the centuries progressed and the city expanded.

One of the oldest buildings still surviving in Glasnevin is the Washerwoman's Hill Restaurant at Glasnevin Hill, which was built in 1700 by Hugo Bath. It takes its name from the old washhouse which once stood on the hill, catering for the needs of those in the fine houses in the area.

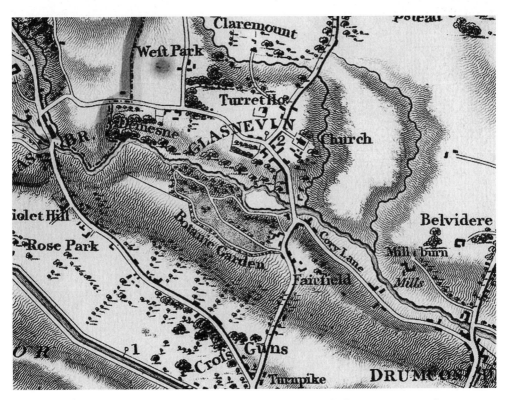

Early nineteenth-century map of Glasnevin. (Courtesy of Glasnevin Heritage)

In the eighteenth century, Glasnevin became a fashionable area for the prosperous classes and Dublin's literary circle, its most famous resident at that time being Dr Patrick Delany, friend of Dean Jonathan Swift, famous author of *Gulliver's Travels, Drapier's Letters* and much more. His name is given to a bridge over the River Tolka, close to Delville House, where he was a frequent visitor. The Bon Secours Hospital is a private hospital owned by the Bon Secours Sisters. It was built on the site of Delville House.

In the nineteenth century, many institutions, mainly educational, were established in the area, as well as the beautiful and impressive Botanic Gardens with its unique range of glasshouses. It is still popular today with tourists and locals and attracts thousands of visitors every year. The nineteenth century also saw the foundation of Glasnevin Cemetery, Ireland's national cemetery. The 180-year-old cemetery represents the national heritage, with people

A map of Glasnevin 'Lower', *c.* 1750. See the distinct round shape of the old 'Inkbottle' school built twenty years earlier. Next to the school a forgotten stream flows into the Tolka. It appears to cross over the road where the entrance to the Botanic Gardens now stands. Further downstream on the Tolka, Drumcondra Mill is marked, on the present Millbourne Avenue. Other points of interest marked are: Fairfield and its landscaped gardens where the BOI and Daneswell Road now stands. Glasnevin Lodge, now the site of the Addison Lodge. The village of Cross Guns (now Hart's Corner). 'Sluts End' on the Finglas Road approximately where 'the Willows' and Claremount Court now are. (Courtesy of Glasnevin Heritage)

from all walks of life buried there. It is the largest cemetery in Ireland, with more than 1.2 million graves. The cemetery was founded in 1832 by Daniel O'Connell, who wanted people of all religions to be buried together. Daniel O'Connell is buried in the cemetery and there is a very tall Round Tower over his grave which was built in 1869.

Thanks to the gardens and cemetery, Glasnevin retained its 'pastoral nature' for the remainder of the century, being spared the extensive housing development which took place throughout Dublin's south side.

With the inclusion of the Drumcondra, Clonliffe and Glasnevin townships within the city boundaries in 1900, the development of Glasnevin took off. New neighbourhoods sprung up and the area soon became a hive of activity from a social, cultural, educational and recreational point of view.

Today, as well as the amenities of the magnificent National Botanic Gardens and local parks, Met Éireann, the Fisheries Board, the National Standards Authority of Ireland, Sustainable Energy Ireland, the National Metrology Laboratory (NML), the Department of Defence and the national enterprise and trade board Enterprise Ireland are all located in the area.

The beautiful redbrick roads, the quaint and attractive old squares, its historic pubs and fine, distinctive churches and its sporting, musical and educational influences make Glasnevin an extraordinary delight and experience for visitors.

1

A BRIEF HISTORY –
FROM ST MOBHI
TO THE TOWNSHIP

Legend has it that Glasnevin was founded by St Mobhi (sometimes known as St Berchan) in the sixth century when he established a monastery on the north bank of the River Tolka. Consequently, Glasnevin merited a place in the *Annals of the Four Masters*, because of his decision. Monks who studied there reputedly included Canice, Comgall and Ciaran. St Columba (or St Columcille) of Iona is thought to have studied under St Mobhi, but left Glasnevin following an outbreak of plague and journeyed north, founding a monastery at Derry.

A settlement grew up around St Mobhi's monastery, which survived until the Viking invasions in the ninth century. Due to its fertile soil, it became one of the farms for Christ Church Cathedral, built in 1028 by Sigtrygg Silkenbeard. By the time of the Normans in around 1200 it was part of Finglas Abbey under Laurence O'Toole, the first Irish Archbishop of Dublin, still a Norse city. In 1240, a church and tower were reconstructed on the site of St Mobhi's monastic church. By 1541, Christ Church was known as the Priory of the Holy Trinity and was amongst the wealthiest churches in Ireland and still had lands in Glasnevin.

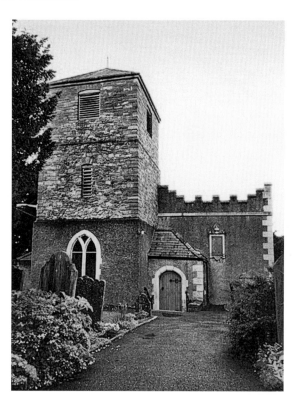

St Mobhi's church,
Glasnevin.
(Courtesy of Nannson/
Dublinforums.net/
St Mobhi's church)

Today, this early monastic influence is well remembered. St Mobhi's church is still being used. The longest street in Glasnevin is Iona Road and the church there is called St Columba's. There is also St Canice's Road and St Columba's Road. In June 1963, the parish of St Columba commemorated the 1,400th anniversary of the departure of the saint from Derry to Iona.

KING BRIAN BORU AND THE 'BLOODY ACRE' FIELD

The Battle of Clontarf was fought on the banks of the River Tolka on Good Friday in 1014. It is almost certain that Brian Boru and his troops set up camp in the Glasnevin area, before crossing the river for the bloody battle. Indeed, there is a field here called the Bloody Acre which is said to mark the site of some of the fighting. The Irish defeated the Danes in a battle in which 7,000 Danes and 4,000 Irish died. However, the king was killed in his moment of triumph. There is a commemorative painting of King Brian Boru on the external wall of Hedigan's Brian Boru pub, just near Cross Guns Bridge on Prospect Road.

The late eleventh and early thirteenth centuries saw the Normans (who had conquered England and Wales in the eleventh century) invade Ireland. As local rulers continued fighting amongst themselves, the Norman King of England, Henry II, was invited to intervene. He arrived in 1171, took control of much land, and then parcelled it out amongst his supporters. Glasnevin ended up under the jurisdiction of Finglas Abbey and Laurence O'Toole, Archbishop of Dublin, took responsibility for it. It subsequently became the property the Holy Trinity (Christ Church Cathedral).

In 1240, a church and tower was reconstructed on the site of the monastery of St Mobhi. The returns of the church for 1326 stated that twenty-eight tenants resided in Glasnevin. The church was enlarged in 1346 and a small hall, known as the Manor Hall, was built. The Holy Faith Convent is now on the site.

HENRY VIII AND THE REFORMATION

When Henry VIII broke from Rome in what is known as the Reformation, an era of religious repression began. During the Dissolution of the Monasteries, Catholic Church property and land was appropriated to the new Church of England, and monasteries (including the one at Glasnevin) were forcibly closed and fell into ruin.

By this stage Glasnevin had developed as a village, with its principal landmark and focal point being its 'bull-ring', noted in 1542.

THE PLANTATION OF IRELAND
AND THIEVES AND ROGUES

The seventeenth- and eighteenth-century plantations of Ireland saw the settlement of Protestant English families on land previously held by Catholics. Lands at Glasnevin were leased to such families and the Protestant church of St Mobhi was rebuilt to facilitate the new residents. The attached churchyard became a graveyard for both Protestants and Catholics. It is still in use to this day and it is said that Robert Emmet is buried there. This claim, however, is made because somebody working in the graveyard once dug up a headless body.

During the seventeenth century, the parishes that had been created in the thirteenth century were subdivided into townlands for land registration purposes. Names such as Clonmel, Draycott's Farm, Forster's Farm, Gough's Farm, Seven Farms and Wycombe's Farm were adopted. Later other names such as Ballygall (town of the foreigner), Bankfarm, Botanic Gardens, Claeremont, Crossguns, Glasnevin Demesne, Hampstead, Prospect and Slutsend were used. Tolkapark, Violethill and Walnutgrove were similarly used. By 1667 Glasnevin had expanded – but not by very much; it is recorded as containing twenty-four houses.

The development of the village was given fresh impetus when Sir John Rogerson built his country residence, 'The Glen' or 'Glasnevin House', outside the village. Rogerson was a shipping merchant, a leading Dublin citizen, an MP and later Lord Mayor. He had purchased Glasnevin Demesne and enlarged the house as a country residence for his family. By the time of his death in 1724, quite a few big houses had been built in the area.

By now Glasnevin was an area for families of distinction – in spite of a comment attributed to the Protestant Archbishop King of Dublin that 'when any couple had a mind to be wicked, they would retire to Glasnevin'. In a letter dated 1725, he described Glasnevin as:

the receptacle for thieves and rogues. The first search when anything was stolen was there, and when any couple had a mind to retire to be wicked there was their harbour. But since the church was built, and service regularly settled, all these evils are banished. Good houses are built in it, and the place civilised.

FAMILIES OF DISTINCTION

Glasnevin had by the eighteenth and nineteenth centuries become a place of some distinction, with a prosperous community. By this time, nearly 1,000 people lived in the village and the surrounding area. According to *Lewis's Topographical Dictionary for Ireland*, published in 1837:

This place, which is pleasantly situated on the northern bank of the river Tolka, was, early in the last century, the residence of many families of distinction, and of several of the most eminent literary characters of that age; and from its proximity to the metropolis it is still the residence of many highly respectable families.

He pointed out that, among the more distinguished of its earlier inhabitants were:

Tickell, Addison, Jonathan Swift, Delany, Steele, Richard Brinsley Sheridan, and Rev. Parnell. The demesne of the first-named is now the site of the botanical gardens of the Royal Dublin Society, and a large apartment of the house is appropriated as the lecture-room of that institution. Delville, formerly the seat of the Rev. Dr. Delany, Dean of Down and Professor in Trinity College Dublin, and then the residence of S. Gordon, Esq.

It was the frequent haunt of Dean Swift and other distinguished literary men of that day. Lewis noted that:

It was pleasantly situated on the banks of the Tolka; on an eminence in the grounds is a temple decorated with paintings by Mrs. Delany, and a medallion bust of Mrs. Johnson, the 'Stella' of Swift.

Engraving of Jonathan Swift (1667–1745) after a painting by Charles Jervas. (Courtesy of Apic/Getty Images)

He also pointed out that:

> On the opposite side of the Tolka was the celebrated seat and demesne of Mitchel, then the residence of the Bishop of Kildare; a little beyond it was Hampstead, formerly the residence of Sir Richard Steele, subsequently that of the late Judge Parsons, and then the seat of B. O'Gorman, Esq.; and in the contiguous parish of Finglas, was the residence of Parnell, formerly vicar of that parish ... In the village are many handsome houses, of which the principal are those of Capt. J. A. Crawford, the Rev. W. C. Roberts, the Rev. R. Walsh (one of the editors of the *History of Dublin*), Capt. R. Smyth, W. Marrable, Esq., T. Howard, Esq., G. Alker, Esq., and Fairfield, the residence of the Rev. J. Hutton.

DELVILLE, THE DEAN AND THE BONS

At the start of the eighteenth century (around 1722), a large house, Delville House, was built on the site of the present Bon Secours Hospital. The house and gardens covered 11 acres. It was originally called Heldeville, which was an amalgamation of the surnames of two of its tenants, Dr Helsam and Dr Patrick Delany, both Fellows of Trinity College. When Delany married his first wife he acquired sole ownership, but it became famous as the home of Delany and his second wife, Mary Pendarves. She was a widow whom Delany married in 1743, and was an accomplished letter writer and influential figure in Irish landscaping.

The couple were friends of the Dean, Jonathan Swift, and, through him, of Alexander Pope. Pope encouraged the Delanys to develop a garden in a style then becoming popular in England – moving away from the very formal, geometric layout that was common. He redesigned the house in the style of a villa and had the gardens laid out in the latest Dutch fashion, creating what was almost certainly Ireland's first naturalistic garden. Mrs Delany (1700–1788) lived long enough to see the change from the formal style to the picturesque. She was important in promoting the idea of 'landscape as painting'. The gardens also contained orange and pear trees and had a small deer-grazing area.

Bushe Delin.ᵗ Aug.ᵗ 1754.   A View of Delville from beyond the Ever-Green Grove.

A view of Delville House from beyond the Ever Green Grove. This is a side view of Delville by the Kilkenny-born artist Letitia Bushe, made three years before her death in 1757. The 'Ever Green Grove' was in the area now occupied by the car parking area of the Bons Secours Hospital. It is said that one could see out to Howth and down over Dublin Bay from the facing windows. (Courtesy of Glasnevin Heritage)

Delville House by artist Brendan Scally, 1971.

The house, under Mrs Delany, an accomplished letter writer, became a centre of Dublin's intellectual life. Swift is said to have composed many of his campaigning pamphlets, including his 'poison letters' and *Drapier's Letters*, while staying there. These were printed in a press hidden in an outhouse in the grounds of Delville. The main reason for his initial visits however, was to see Delany's niece, Esther Johnson, known affectionately as Stella. Through her correspondence with her sister, Mrs Dewes, Mrs Delany wrote of Swift in 1733: 'he calls himself my master and corrects me when I speak bad English or do not pronounce my words distinctly'. Delville is also significant as the location where much of Swift's satire on Parliament and the injustices perpetuated by it was written, including the following.

On One of the Windows at Delville

A bard, grown desirous of saving his pelf,
Built a house he was sure would hold none but himself.
This enraged god Apollo, who Mercury sent,

And bid him go ask what his votary meant?

'Some foe to my empire has been his adviser:

'Tis of dreadful portent when a poet turns miser!

Tell him, Hermes, from me, tell that subject of mine,

I have sworn by the Styx, to defeat his design;

For wherever he lives, the Muses shall reign;

And the Muses, he knows, have a numerous train.'

Another poem attributed to Jonathan Swift is one called 'Dr Delany's Villa', written around 1722. There is some controversy over the authorship of this poem, with some scholars arguing that, in fact, it was written by Dr Sheridan, a contemporary and friend of Swift. Thomas Sheridan (1687–1738) was an Anglican divine, essayist, playwright, poet, schoolmaster and translator. Either way, it gives a useful picture of the importance of Delville at the time.

Dr Delany's Villa

WOULD you that Delville I describe?

Believe me, sir, I will not gibe:

For who would be satirical

Upon a thing so very small?

You scarce upon the borders enter,

Before you're at the very centre.

A single crow can make it night,

When o'er your farm she takes her flight:

Yet, in this narrow compass, we

Observe a vast variety;

Both walks, walls, meadows, and parterres,

Windows and doors, and rooms and stairs,

And hills and dales, and woods and fields,

And hay, and grass, and corn, it yields;

All to your haggard brought so cheap in,

Without the mowing or the reaping:

A razor, though to say't I'm loth,

Would shave you and your meadows both.

Though small's the farm, yet here's a house

Full large to entertain a mouse;
But where a rat is dreaded more
Than savage Caledonian boar;
For, if it's entered by a rat,
There is no room to bring a cat.
A little rivulet seems to steal
Down through a thing you call a vale,
Like tears adown a wrinkled cheek,
Like rain along a blade of leek:
And this you call your sweet meander,
Which might be suck'd up by a gander,
Could he but force his nether bill
To scoop the channel of the rill.
For sure you'd make a mighty clutter,
Were it as big as city gutter.
Next come I to your kitchen garden,
Where one poor mouse would fare but hard in;
And round this garden is a walk,
No longer than a tailor's chalk;
Thus I compare what space is in it,
A snail creeps round it in a minute.
One lettuce makes a shift to squeeze
Up through a tuft you call your trees:
And, once a year, a single rose
Peeps from the bud, but never blows;
In vain then you expect its bloom!
It cannot blow for want of room.
In short, in all your boasted seat,
There's nothing but yourself that's great.

DELVILLE AND THE BLIND HARPIST

Jonathan Swift was not the only one to write about Delville. The old IR£50
banknote gives us a hint about another unusual connection with Delville
House. Depicted on the note was the blind Irish composer and harpist
Turlough O'Carolan (1670–1738). O'Carolan composed many melodies

and these were often dedicated to named individuals. Over 200 of his compositions still exist. O'Carolan was a visitor to Delville and two of his lesser-known pieces were written for his Glasnevin hosts: *Dr Delany's* and *Mrs Delany's*. Following the death of O'Carolan, his son, also a harpist, came under the patronage of the Delanys. Not as honourable or as good a musician as his father, he absconded to England with a wad of the doctor's money, never to be seen again.

Patrick Delany died in 1768, at the age of 82, prompting his widow to sell Delville and return to her native England, where she lived until her death twenty years later. Subsequently it became the home of Stephen Lanigan O'Keefe.

The house was demolished in 1946–7 by the Mercy nuns and the Bon Secours Hospital was built on the site. Just prior to its demolition, local artist

ERECTED
BY THE DESIRE OF SYDNEY LADY MORGAN
TO THE MEMORY OF
CAROLAN
THE LAST OF THE IRISH BARDS

OBIIT
A D MDCCXXXVIII AETATIS SVAE AN LXVIII

Turlough O'Carolan in St Patrick's Cathedral, Dublin. The blind harpist was a frequent visitor to Delville. (Courtesy of St Patrick's Cathedral/ Michael Pegum)

Turlough O'Carolan,
the blind harpist.
(Courtesy of GCI/Armstrong)

Brendan Scally made a drawing of Delville House, with Glasnevin stream in the foreground. This is in the National Library of Ireland. He called his drawing 'The Beginning of the End'.

The Delville name lives on in Glasnevin with Delville Road.

FROM THE LINDSAY FAMILY TO THE GLASNEVIN TOWNSHIP

Sir John Rogerson, the shipping magnate, politician, entrepreneur and developer after whom a River Liffey quay is named, built Glasnevin House, which was subsequently occupied by Charles Lindsay, Bishop of Kildare and Leighlin. Years later, he and a William John sold their holdings of Rogerson's lands at Glasnevin (including Glasnevin House) to George Hayward Lindsay. This transfer included the sum of £1,500. Although the transaction does not specifically cite the marriage of George Hayward Lindsay to Lady Mary Catherine Gore, Lindsay almost certainly came into the lands at Glasnevin as a result of his marriage. Eventually the property passed to Revd Charles Dalrymple Lindsay (1760–1846), the sixth and youngest son of the 30th Lord Lindsay of Crawford.

Today, the Lindsay family is remembered in two roads in the area – Lindsay and Crawford. When Charles died, the house and gardens were sold to the Holy Faith nuns, who have been in Glasnevin since.

CROSSING THE CANALS TO GLASNEVIN

At the end of the nineteenth century, Glasnevin's Botanic Gardens were at the very edge of Dublin City; most Dubliners resided between the two canals. There were vast tracts of vacant land in Glasnevin and adjacent areas. Griffith Avenue, for example, was only developed in the 1920s. Health considerations also ruled out housing developments in some parts of the city and suburbs. Living close to a cemetery – in this case Glasnevin Cemetery – was seen as posing a health risk.

However, by the 1860s, circumstances were forcing Dublin's middle classes to move beyond the canal boundaries. The influx of famine victims into the city, higher city taxes and a wish to be separated from the lower classes precipitated the building and development boom from the 1860s. Property developers were quick to take advantage of the new situation and roads were laid out in Glasnevin. When Drumcondra began to rapidly expand in the 1870s, the residents of Glasnevin sought to protect their district and opposed being merged with the neighbouring suburb. Drumcondra needed to become a township with independent control over its own water supply, as the City Fathers had turned down its proposal for a drainage scheme for the area because it was situated on the banks of the River Tolka. The burgeoning Glasnevin also needed a good water supply and it was suggested that the two districts were amalgamated. One of the objectors to the proposed amalgamation was the property owner Dr Gogarty, the father of the Irish poet, Oliver St John Gogarty. However, after much negotiation, and with the support of the Catholic Church (because of Clonliffe College and All Hallows College), Glasnevin became a township in 1879 as part of the Drumcondra, Clonliffe and Glasnevin Township, represented by five, five and four commissioners respectively. This gave the area (and the property developers) some control over water, lighting and other local amenities, and the arrangement appealed to many of the residents. House construction also accelerated in the early years of the new township.

Twenty years later, the township became part of the City of Dublin and in 1900, under the Dublin Boundaries Act, it received Royal Assent on 6 August. By this time, the Dublin Corporation had decided to extend its boundaries for financial reasons and thus absorb the township into the city. The residents, however, strongly opposed its abolition, even though the township did not have the resources to cope with any further expansion of the area.

George Hayward Lindsay's eldest son, Lieutenant Colonel Henry Gore Lindsay, was in possession of his father's lands at Glasnevin when the area began to be developed at the beginning of the twentieth century. The development of his lands after 1903/04 marked the start of the gradual expansion of the area.

Glasnevin remained relatively undeveloped until the opening up of the Carroll Estate in 1914, which saw the creation of the redbrick residential roads, e.g. Iona Road and Lindsay Road, running down towards Drumcondra. The process was accelerated by Dublin Corporation in the 1920s and the present shape of the suburb was firmly in place by 1930. Nevertheless, until comparatively recent years, a short stroll up the Old Finglas Road brought you rapidly into open countryside.

2

THE BOTS –
THE NATIONAL
BOTANIC GARDENS

Glasnevin is home to Dublin's magnificent National Botanic Gardens. Botanical gardens were originally developed on behalf of the medical profession, who recognised the curative properties of plants. It was held that an organised system, rather than collecting plants from the wild, would be the way forward.

In 1733, the poet Thomas Tickell had bought Teeling's Tenement. He was a man of letters who was secretary to the Lord Justices in the Privy Council of Ireland, a post he retained until his death in 1740. Henry Addison, famous litterateur and essayist, was a friend of Tickell and he was secretary to the Lord Lieutenant. He was also a keen gardener. Addison loved Tickell's gardens and had a favourite walk there that became known as 'Addison's Walk'.

'THE BRIGHTEST JEWEL' – WHY THE GARDENS?

In 1790, the Irish Parliament (Grattan's Parliament), with the active support of the Speaker of the House, John Foster, granted funds to the Dublin Society (now the Royal Dublin Society), to establish a public botanic garden. Before this, the gardens of Trinity College would have been used for research purposes, but with the land being needed for buildings, Dr Walter Wade, Professor of Botany in Trinity, had petitioned parliament for a public botanic garden. The house and lands of Thomas Tickell had been sold earlier in the year to the Irish Parliament and so these were given to the Dublin Society for them to establish Ireland's first Botanic Gardens, to 'promote a scientific knowledge in the various branches of agriculture'.

The site was originally 27 acres but was subsequently extended and part of the gardens was originally the natural flood plain of the River Tolka. In 1795, the serious work of the development of the gardens commenced and by 1819, Dr Wade was able to say that 'our botanical establishment [is] the brightest jewel I am proud to say in the Dublin Socyty's [sic] cap ...'

Since the original purpose of the gardens was to promote a scientific approach to the study of agriculture, in its early years the gardens housed plants that were useful for animal and human food and medicine and for dyeing. However, it also grew plants that promoted an understanding of systematic botany or were simply beautiful or interesting in themselves.

Glasshouses at the National Botanic Gardens. (Courtesy of NBG/OPW/GCI)

By the 1830s, the agricultural purpose of the gardens had been overtaken by the pursuit of botanical knowledge. This was facilitated by the arrival of plants from around the world and by closer contact with the great gardens in Britain, notably Kew and Edinburgh, and plant importers such as Messrs Veitch.

By 1838, the basic shape of the gardens had been established. The curator of the gardens, Ninian Niven, had in four years laid out the system of roads and paths and located many of the garden features that are present today.

THE 'UNSURPASSED' INFLUENCE OF DAVID MOORE

Niven's successor was David Moore and his contribution to the gardens, to its plant collections and to its reputation nationally and internationally is unsurpassed. His interests and abilities were wide ranging; he had studied the flora of Antrim and Derry, fungi, algae, lichens, bryophytes, ferns and flowering plants, before taking up his post at Glasnevin. While at Glasnevin, he developed links with botanic gardens in Britain, Europe and Australia (his brother Charles became director at Sydney Botanic Gardens).

Moore used the great interest in plants that existed among the estate owners and owners of large gardens in Ireland to expand trial grounds for rare plants not expected to thrive at Glasnevin. The collections at Kilmacurragh, Headford and Fota, for example, attest to this.

Inside the Botanic Gardens, *c.* 1900. (Courtesy of Robert French/GCI/OPW)

Over the past two centuries, the gardens have played a central role in botanical and horticultural advancement in Ireland. Plants and seeds have been imported and new cultivars and species distributed to gardeners and nurserymen. The fastigate gorse, found at Mount Stewart in 1804, was the first cultivar to be introduced from Glasnevin and this has been followed by numerous others, such as the pampas grass, the pink-flushed lily from Nepal, the beautiful Chatham Island daisy-bush, the exquisitely scented *Abelia triflora*, and the giant lily, *Cardiocrinum giganteum*. In the 1840s, orchids were cultivated from seed to flowering stage for the first time at Glasnevin and it was here, in 1869, that hybridisation of the insectivorous pitcher-plants sarracenia was first carried out successfully.

The soil of the Glasnevin Botanic Gardens is heavy alkaline boulder clay, which confines the growing of calcifuge plants, such as rhododendrons and ericas, to specially prepared peat beds. There are, however, a wide range of habitats within the garden and these are incorporated within a botanical rather than geographical layout. They include special areas devoted to roses, ground cover plants, economic and poisonous plants, native plants and herbs and vegetables. Glasnevin also houses a large rockery, a bog garden, a wild garden and a double, curving herbaceous border, which is a marvellous sight in summer.

THE GREAT FAMINE

It was David Moore who first noted potato blight in Ireland at Glasnevin, on 20 August 1845, and predicted that the impact on the potato crop would lead to famine in Ireland. He continued to investigate the cause of the blight and correctly identified it as a fungus, but narrowly missed finding a remedy.

David Moore was succeeded by his son Frederick, who was made curator at the age of just twenty-two. Some of the gardening establishment figures of the day were sceptical that such a young man would be up to the job. Frederick Moore soon justified his appointment and went on to establish Glasnevin as one of the great gardens of the world. In due course he was knighted for his services to horticulture.

THE DUBLIN IRONMASTER AND THE CURVILINEAR RANGE OF GLASSHOUSES

The glasshouses have long been a great attraction of Glasnevin. Particularly striking are the 400ft-long greenhouses, the famous and magnificent glasshouses known as the Curvilinear Range. They were created by Dublin ironmaster Richard Turner between 1840 and 1869, Turner having successfully persuaded the Royal Dublin Society that a glasshouse made of an iron structure would be a better long-term investment than one made of wood. Twenty years later, Turner ingeniously doubled the building's size by removing the walls and extending it back.

View of glasshouses in Botanic Gardens, *c.* 1900. (Courtesy of Robert French/GCI/NBG)

View of path in the National Botanic Gardens, Glasnevin, early twentieth century. (Courtesy of GCI/NBG)

Richard Turner (1798–1881) was the most important glasshouse designer in Ireland and was responsible for many of the large glasshouses that were so much a part of fashionable development in Victorian Britain. Born in 1798 into a family with long associations with the iron trade, he was an innovative designer, and the high quality and decorative details of his glasshouses were famous throughout Europe. With Decimus Burton, he was responsible for the design and manufacture of the glasshouses at Kew Gardens and the Winter Gardens at Regent's Park. He was also responsible for the

Great Exhibition building of 1853 in Dublin, as well as the original roof of Broadstone Railway Station. His ironworks, the Hammersmith Works, were at Ballsbridge in Dublin, and survived there until the end of the nineteenth century. Turner's firm was singled out by a writer in *The Builder* in 1856 as the 'one great manufacturing house' in the 'slumbering metropolis' of Dublin. He was a pioneer in the structural use of wrought iron. His intuitive grasp of engineering design, and his pioneering skill at producing curved glazing bars of wrought iron to a standard plan gave his buildings their unique style.

Another fine glasshouse in the gardens is the Great Palm House. Built in 1884, it contains a diverse tropical palm tree collection from around the world. It is also notable today for its cycads, giant bamboo, bananas and bromeliads, while its side wings, housing orchids and flowering pot plants. At 20m in height, it is the tallest building in the gardens. In the winter of 1948/9, the renowned philosopher, Ludwig Wittgenstein, lived and worked in Ireland. He frequently came to the Palm House to sit and write. There is a plaque commemorating him on the steps he sat on. Ireland's former Taoiseach, Bertie Ahern, lived nearby and was a frequent visitor to the 'Bots', as he referred to them. Many times he would be seen walking along any of the numerous pathways in the gardens, doubtlessly contemplating matters of State in such magnificent and inspiring surroundings.

VICTORIA AND THE AMAZON WATER LILY

Such was Turner's renown and his glasshouses a wonder to behold, that when Queen Victoria visited Ireland in the 1850s, she called in to the Botanic Gardens to see his work.

When the Curvilinear Range was restored to its former glory in 1995, the bicentenary of the gardens, a concert by Michael Holohan was held in one of the glasshouses to celebrate the occasion. Guest of honour was Nobel Laureate, the poet Seamus Heaney. Local poets who had written about the gardens, and the famous Glasnevin-based Lindsay Singers under Ethna Barror, also featured in the concert.

Of the glasshouses themselves, to the right of the main entrance to the gardens, the first range includes the Fern House, built in 1890,

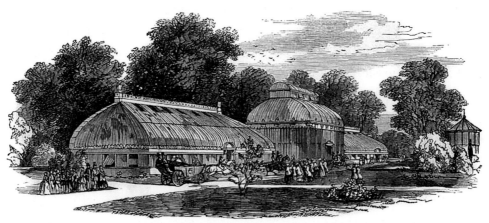

The visit of Queen Victoria and Prince Albert to Glasnevin Botanic Gardens, Glasnevin in 1849 to see the Curvilinear Range of glasshouses. (Courtesy of Nansson/Dublinforums.net)

which houses tropical and temperate ferns. It is a rather dull aluminium glasshouse, constructed in 1966 to replace an attractive Victorian octagonal conservatory. This Fern House is divided into separate compartments for tree ferns and tropical species. Here, amidst dense foliage, the visitor will find the native but rare Killarney fern, *Trichomanes speciosum*, and the Australian tree fern, *Todea barbara*, which had been transferred here in 1969 from the old Trinity College Botanic Gardens and is reputed to be 400 years old.

In summer, the Aquatic or Victoria House, which was built in 1854 to hold and protect the gigantic Amazon waterlily, which is grown from seed each year. At that time it was only recently introduced and was one of the wonders of the age.

The Cactus and Succulent House, built in 1890, contains both the American cacti as well as the unrelated but cactus-like spurges from Africa.

The Curvilinear Range tells the story of conifers in the central house. The west wing of the range contains an extensive collection of rhododendrons from south-east Asia. The east wing contains plants from Australia, South Africa and South America which evolved from ancient flora.

The Palm House Range, built in 1884, was restored in 2004. The walls are constructed from teak bound by wrought iron.

The Orchid House contains modern hybrids, as well as an important collection of special orchids, many of which have been recently collected in Belize.

Although the gardens at Glasnevin are more than 200 years old, very few of the trees and shrubs were planted more than a century ago. One of the older plants is the Chusan palm, *Trachycarpus fortunei*, planted outside the Curvilinear Range in 1870. Other majestic, patriarchal trees are a *Cedrus atlantantica* 'Pendula', planted some time before 1877, and a large *Zelkova carpinifolia* that looks especially good in winter.

MORE HIGHLIGHTS FROM THE GARDENS

A remarkable early Victorian chain tent draped with a venerable wisteria is not to be missed – years ago it had a weeping ash growing in the centre but this has long since been replaced with a steel pole. One of the most popular sights in the garden, however, is the 'Last Rose of Summer' – a cultivar of the China rose *R. chinensis* 'Old Blush'. It was raised from a cutting taken from a rose at Jenkinstown House in County Kilkenny which, according to tradition, was the rose that inspired Thomas Moore to write his famous ballad, 'The Last Rose of Summer'.

The gardens border Glasnevin Cemetery. The Glasnevin Gateway, an interlinking gateway between Glasnevin (Prospect) Cemetery and the gardens, opened in late 2013. Restoration work over the past few decades has enhanced the natural beauty of the gardens and made them a premier national attraction.

The gardens today include a vegetable garden and a rose garden, and the double line of yew trees known as Addison's Walk still survives from the early days of the gardens. Aside from the glasshouses, the grounds include an arboretum of various specimen trees, annual displays and herbaceous borders, a pond and a burren area that recreates the beauty of the plants in north-western County Clare. The 'What is Life' sculpture was designed by Charles Jencks and celebrates the 60th anniversary of the discovery of the DNA double helix in 1953.

Local historian Tony O'Doherty states that the original entrance to the gardens included a pair of Doric cottages. By 1820, they had been replaced by two 'lodges'. In the 1890s, the two lodges were altered to what are the present striking buildings now standing either side of the entrance gates. The turnstile (with 'The Elliptical Improved Patent' printed on it) was invented by the manufacturer C. Isler & Co., of London sometime after 1880, so we presume that the gates date from around the same time. Alterations to the gates, either by replacement or additions, occurred since then as the gardens, once known as the Royal Botanic Gardens, were later renamed the National Botanic Gardens and the appropriate lettering in English and Irish were added. It would appear from the turnstiles that at one time visitors had to pay an entrance fee to view the gardens.

THE FUTURE

Today the gardens grow over 300 endangered species from around the world, and six species that are already extinct in the wild. The arboretum, pond, river banks, cultivar collections, vegetable garden, glasshouses and wildlife provide much interest. The National Herbarium, based within the gardens, has a collection of nearly three quarters of a million dried plant specimens. It also has an active DNA research laboratory.

The Botanic Gardens came into State care in 1878 and since then have been administered variously by the Department of Art and Industry, the Department of Agriculture, Dúchas the Heritage Service of the Department of Arts, Heritage the Gaeltacht and the Islands, and the Office of Public Works (OPW), which currently has responsibility for the gardens.

A development plan for the gardens, published in 1992, led to a dramatic programme of restoration and renewal. Primary amongst these was the magnificent restoration of the Turner Curvilinear Range of glasshouses, completed for the bicentenary of the Garden in 1995. A new purpose-built herbarium/library was opened in 1997 and the eighteenth-century Director's House and the Curator's House have been refurbished. New service glasshouses and compost storage bays have been built also been built and additional lecture rooms for the Teagasc Course in Amenity

Horticulture were opened in 1999. Improved visitor and education facilities have been provided in a new Visitor Centre.

In tandem with the restoration and expansion of the buildings, upgrading of the collections and displays has also been in progress. The work of plant identification and classification, of documenting, labelling and publishing continues, as does that of education and service to the visiting public.

3

PROSPECT CEMETERY – GLASNEVIN NATIONAL CEMETERY

Glasnevin is probably best known for its cemetery, Prospect Cemetery – a mixture of Père La Chaise in Paris and Arlington National Cemetery in the United States. On approaching the cemetery, one is met with high walls of best Dublin calp around the old cemetery perimeter, interspersed at intervals with tall, battlemented towers. The cemetery led to Glasnevin being known as 'the dead centre of Dublin'. In deference to the nearby Croke Park GAA stadium, it is also known as 'Croak Park'!

EARLY HISTORY OF PROSPECT – THE ROLE OF DANIEL O'CONNELL, THE LIBERATOR

Since the Reformation of the sixteenth century, all Catholic churches and churchyards had become the property of the Established Church of King Henry VIII. It became an increasingly contentious issue that Catholics continued to be buried in such grounds and in many cases without a Catholic burial service. By 1823, the question of Catholic burial had become part of Daniel O'Connell's campaign for Catholic Emancipation and he felt the only solution was to establish a Catholic burial ground. However, he stipulated that it was to be open to all denominations and that clergy of different faiths would officiate at the relevant burial services. The first Dublin Cemeteries' Committee, responsible for the management of these new cemeteries, was formed from the members of O'Connell's Catholic Association. Although the first cemetery was opened on 15 October 1829 in Goldenbridge in Dublin, it was from this movement and in this climate that Prospect Cemetery, Glasnevin was founded.

In July 1831, land adjacent to the Botanic Gardens was bought from Revd Charles Lindsay. The site was ideal as it was close to Dublin City but outside the boundary. It was initially named Prospect Cemetery, a name chosen from the townland of Prospect which surrounded the cemetery lands, and was consecrated by Monsignor Yore in September 1831. It was opened to the public for the first time on 21 February 1832 and the first burial, that of 4-year-old Michael Casey from Francis Street in Dublin's Liberties, took place on the following day in a section of the cemetery known as Curran's Square.

Appendix

VAULTS.—GLASNEVIN CEMETERY.

		ft. ft.	£ s. d.
O'Connell Tower,	Furnished with solid cast metal doors, iron gates, with lattice wire, locks, etc., and the surface of vaults completed with best Wicklow granite cut stone,	8 by 8	200 0 0
			150 0 0
O'Connell Circle,		,,	
Along Walks		8 ,, 6	45 0 0
Do.		8 ,, 4	33 0 0

Bodies proposed to be placed in vaults purchased since July, 1871, must be enclosed in leaden coffins.

FEES FOR INTERMENT.

To be paid in addition to charges for vaults or ground, etc., purchased in perpetuity.

	Each Adult.	Child under 12 years.
	£ s. d.	£ s. d.
In New Chapel Section—		
Private vault	3 0 0	2 0 0
St. Brigid's Section—South and first borders in Dublin division of such section	3 0 0	2 0 0
O'Connell Circle Ground (also Chapel Circle, Golden Bridge)	2 0 0	1 10 0
Curran's Square, Chapel Circle	1 10 0	1 0 0
South Section—		
First, second, and third border plots ...	1 10 0	1 0 0
Fourth and all others	0 17 6	0 10 0
East, West (Dublin Section—		
First and second border plots	1 10 0	1 0 0
First border plots (also Barrack section) ...	1 2 6	0 12 6
Second and all other plots (also in Canal Section)	0 17 6	0 10 0
Garden Section (Vicinity of O'Connell Circle)—		
First border plots	1 10 0	1 0 0
Other first border plots	1 2 6	0 12 6
Second border plots	0 17 6	0 10 0 ·
All others	0 12 6	0 6 6
St. Brigid's Section—		
Second borders in Dublin division, and first and second borders in Garden division ...	1 10 0	1 0 0
All others in Dublin division	1 2 6	0 12 6
Third and all others in Garden division ..	1 2 6	0 12 6
Common graves in Old Section, non-vested ground	0 15 0	0 8 0
Common graves in New Section, non-vested ground	1 2 6	0 12 6

POOR.

		Each Body.
		£ s. d.
Government and other Public Institutions, Coroner's cases	... ...	0 5 0
(except in latter case, when interred by members of deceased's family, then the charge is only 1s. 6d.)		
The general public	... ...	0 1 6

The late nineteenth-century burial fees at Glasnevin Cemetery. (Courtesy of Glasnevin Trust/GCI)

View of Glasnevin and cemetery, early twentieth century. (Courtesy of GCI)

Originally covering 9 acres of ground, the area of the cemetery has now grown to approximately 124 acres. This includes its expansion on the southern side of the Finglas Road with the section called St Paul's. The option of cremation has been provided since March 1982. The majority of those interred are ordinary Dubliners, but many are well known for the part they have played in Irish history and for the contribution they have made to Irish politics, religion and culture. The cemetery, therefore, has an important place in the evolution of our country, and the manner of its establishment in 1832 is of historical significance.

CHAPELS AND CUBAN BLOODHOUNDS

The first architect of the cemetery was Patrick Byrne (1783–1864). Chosen because of his associations with the Catholic Committee and patronised by the Catholic clergy, he later became well known for the design of St Paul's church on Arran Quay, St Audoen's on High Street, the church of the Three Patrons in Rathgar and several other churches in the city environs and surrounding counties.

Patrick Byrne designed the layout of the grounds and the enclosing walls. These walls had many watchtowers, a necessary requirement because of the high incidence of bodysnatching at this period. Cuban bloodhounds patrolled the cemetery as an additional precaution. The original entrance was located in Prospect Square, where Byrne designed the beautiful neoclassical entrance gate, the cemetery office and the sexton's residence.

He was also responsible for the first ecclesiastical building in the grounds, a temple of neoclassical design which he later adapted to become the first mortuary chapel. This building was situated in an area of the cemetery known as the Old Chapel Circle, which contains the grave where Patrick Byrne himself was interred in 1864. James Joseph McCarthy RHA (1817–1882), a follower of Augustus Pugin, designed the present-day entrance gates and offices on the Finglas Road and also the Mortuary Chapel.

FROM PROSPECT TO GLASNEVIN

Today over 1 million men and women are laid to rest in Glasnevin Cemetery. This unique Victorian burial place is Ireland's National Cemetery, because so many who were instrumental in the history of the country are memorialised here. It is the final resting place of the men and women who have helped shape Ireland's past and present.

These include:

Thomas Ashe – Mayor of Dublin who died on hunger strike in 1917 in the post-1916 Rising build-up to the War of Independence.

Kevin Barry – an 18-year-old medical student executed by the British for his role in the Irish War of Independence. (His body was moved from Mountjoy Prison to Glasnevin in October 2001, having been accorded a State funeral.)

Piaras Béaslaí – Easter Rising survivor turned writer/biographer of Michael Collins.

The scene at the graveside of Thomas Ashe in Glasnevin Cemetry. Michael Collins gave the briefest of orations. His words were: 'Nothing additional remains to be said. That volley which we have heard is the only speech which is proper to make above the grave of a dead Fenian'. (Courtesy of GHS)

Firing Party at funeral of Joseph McGuinness in Glasnevin Cemetery, 2 June 1922. (Courtesy of Irish Volunteers Commemorative Committee)

Alfred Chester Beatty – buried here in 1968, Chester Beatty was North American by birth but Irish by descent, and made his fortune in mining. He was known for his collections of rare books and art, including a rare Oriental collection of artefacts, books, paintings and manuscripts, which can be seen at Dublin Castle in the Chester Beatty Library.

Brendan Behan – author and playwright, his best-known works are *Borstal Boy* and *The Quare Fellow*. He was a colourful, well-known Dublin character; his personal dedication to an independent Ireland popularised him and he was one of the country's most widely recognised post-Second World War writers.

Ernest Blythe – politician and Abbey Theatre Director for thirty years.

Professor Thomas Bodkin – lawyer, art historian, art collector and curator.

Harry Boland – friend of Michael Collins and anti-Treaty politician; a key figure in reorganising the Irish Volunteers after 1916.

Alicia Brady – one of the last casualties of the 1913 Dublin Lockout. The 16-year-old died on 1 January and her funeral took place in Glasnevin Cemetery on 4 January 1914.

Christy Brown – paralysed from birth, he was the writer of *My Left Foot* and subject of the film of the same name. He also wrote *Down All the Days*. He used the toes of his left foot to write and paint.

Father Francis Browne – Jesuit priest and renowned photographer who took the last known photographs of the ill-fated liner *Titanic*.

Cathal Brugha – first President of Dáil Éireann (January – April 1919), he was killed in the Civil War.

Margaret Burke – opera singer.

Thomas Henry Burke – Permanent Under Secretary to Chief Secretary for Ireland, Lord Frederick Cavendish, he was shot along with Cavendish in the Phoenix Park murders in 1882. The Resident Magistrates of Ireland erected an additional memorial to him in the cemetery.

Alfie Byrne – nine times Lord Mayor of Dublin in the 1930s and '40s, he was known as the 'shaking hand of Dublin'.

Sergeant James Byrne – Victoria Cross recipient (Indian Mutiny).

John Keegan Casey – mid-nineteenth-century songwriter who wrote poems and songs for the Fenian Movement, including 'The Rising of the Moon'.

Roger Casement – human rights campaigner turned Irish revolutionary, he was involved in the 1916 Rising and was executed for treason in 1916 at Pentonville Prison. His remains were transferred back to Ireland in the 1960s, where he was given a State funeral.

Robert Erskine Childers – Irish Nationalist and writer, executed by the Irish Free State government during the Irish Civil War. He wrote best-selling book *The Riddle of the Sands*.

Mary 'Molly' Alden Childers – Irish Nationalist and wife of Robert Erskine Childers.

J. J. Clancy – Irish Nationalist MP (1847–1928).

Michael Collins – the renowned and charismatic leader of the Irish Volunteers/Irish Republican Army in the Irish War of Independence, he ordered fourteen British undercover agents to be executed on 21 November 1920. In response, British forces killed twelve spectators at a football game in Croke Park. Collins helped to negotiate the Anglo-Irish Treaty of 1921, which saw the establishment of the Irish Free State in 1922 and was the first internationally recognised Irish head of government. Shortly afterwards, he died in an ambush in the Civil War at the young age of 32.

Crowds at Glasnevin for the burial of Michael Collins. (UCC Cultural Multitext)

Funeral cortège of Michael Collins passing through O'Connell Street on the way to Glasnevin Cemetery. (UCC Cultural Multitext)

Michael Collin's coffin being carried into Glasnevin Cemetery, 28 August 1922.
(UCC Cultural Multitext)

People arriving at Glasnevin for the burial of Michael Collins, 1922. (UCC Cultural Multitext)

President of the Executive Council, W.T. Cosgrave, and mourners at the graveside in Glasnevin Cemetery for the burial of Michael Collins.

Roddy Connolly – socialist politician and son of James Connolly.

Margaret Craig – renowned Abbey actress who died in 1972.

Jack Cruise – hugely popular comedian and entertainer, much associated with the Gaiety Theatre. Died in 1979.

John Philpot Curran – patriotic barrister, renowned wit, lawyer on behalf of Wolfe Tone and other United Irishmen, Sarah Curran's father (she was the girlfriend of Robert Emmet). Died 1817 and his remains were transferred to Dublin in 1834, when he was buried by torchlight.

Michael Cusack – considered the founder of the Gaelic Athletic Association (GAA). He died in 1906.

Michael Dargan – philanthropist.

William Dargan – Ireland's rail pioneer and architect, responsible for the laying of the first rail line in Ireland. He also planned and paid for the National Gallery of Ireland.

Charlotte Despard – Irish feminist.

Éamon de Valera – twice President of Ireland and Taoiseach (Prime Minister) seven times, he was a leader of the movement for independence during the 1916 Rising. After his sentence of death was commuted, he was imprisoned for treason. He fought in the War of Independence and Civil War, formed the Fianna Fail political party, crafted the 1937 Constitution of Ireland and led the government for decades, shaping the nation into a reflection of many of his own beliefs and visions.

Sinéad de Valera – wife of Éamon de Valera, buried in the same plot.

Anne Devlin – famed housekeeper of Robert Emmet. She was arrested after the 1803 rebellion but refused to betray Emmet's secrets, despite being tortured. Her headstone includes the words: '... faithful servant to Robert Emmet, who possessed some rare and noble qualities, who lived in obscurity and poverty and so died in 1851.'

John Devoy – Fenian leader, he made his name in Irish American politics and was described as the 'greatest of the Fenians' by P.H. Pearse. He died in 1928.

John Blake Dillon – Irish writer and Young Ireland politician, he co-founded *The Nation* newspaper.

Patrick Dinneen – producer of the highly-respected *Irish-English Dictionary*, he died in 1934.

Martin Doherty – IRA member.

Frank Duff – founder of the Legion of Mary.

Edward Duffy – Irish Fenian, Irish Republican Brotherhood.

Charles Gavan Duffy – Young Irelander and co-founder of *The Nation* newspaper with Thomas Davis and John Dillon. After imprisonment with Daniel O'Connell, he emigrated to Australia, where he became Prime Minister of Victoria. His remains were interred in Glasnevin after his death in 1903.

Private Thomas Duffy – VC recipient (Indian Mutiny).

James Duffy – bookseller and founder of the Popular Sixpenny Library, he died in 1871.

Ben Dunne – founder of the Dunnes Stores chain of supermarkets, he died in 1983.

Thomas Addis Emmet – grandnephew of Robert Emmet.

James Fitzharris – he was in the 'Invincibles' and acted as a jarvey for them. His nickname was 'Skin the Goat'.

James Fitzmaurice – aviation pioneer who was the first to fly the Atlantic from east to west (acting as co-pilot). He died in 1965.

William John Fitzpatrick – nineteenth-century biographer and historian, whose works included *The Sham Squire*.

Grace Gifford – wife of 1916 Rising leader Joseph Mary Plunkett. She married Plunkett on the eve of his execution in Kilmainham Jail. She died in 1955.

Francis Gleeson – Chaplain to the British Army and the Irish Free State.

Edmund Dwyer Gray – Irish nineteenth-century MP and son of Sir John Gray. He was the owner of the *Freeman's Journal* and served as Lord Mayor of Dublin.

Sir John Gray – Irish nineteenth-century MP. His statue adorns Dublin's O'Connell Street.

Maud Gonne – nationalist campaigner, love of W.B. Yeat's life. She was famed for her beauty and was the mother of Nobel and Lenin Peace Prize winner Seán MacBride, who is buried in the grave also.

Arthur Griffith – President of Dáil Éireann (January – August 1922) and founder of Sinn Féin.

Denis Guiney – businessman and owner of Guiney's and Clery's Department Stores in Dublin. He died in 1967.

Arthur Griffith's tricolour-covered coffin is carried through Glasnevin Cemetery. (Courtesy of UCC Cultural Mutiltext)

Funeral cortège of Arthur Griffith, founder of Sinn Féin, en route to Glasnevin Cemetery, August 1922. Griffith Avenue in Glasnevin is named after him. (UCC Cultural Multitext)

Timothy Harrington – prominent in the Land League and founder and editor of the *Kerry Sentinel*, represented Westmeath and Dublin in Parliament for the Irish Parliamentary Party and served as Lord Mayor of Dublin.

Joseph Patrick Haverty – Irish painter.

Tim Healy – First Governor-General of the Irish Free State. He was the first to call Parnell the 'uncrowned King of Ireland'.

Denis Caulfield Heron – lawyer and politician.

Gerard Manley Hopkins – poet.

Stanislaus Joyce and Mary Joyce – parents of James Joyce, author of *Ulysses* and other famous works.

Peadar Kearney – composer of the Irish National Anthem, *Amhrán na bhFiann*.

John Kelly – Land Leaguer and Home Ruler, imprisoned many times for his activities.

Luke Kelly – singer and folk musician and founding member of The Dubliners.

William Nicholas Keogh – Judge much reviled in the late nineteenth century for trials of Fenians. It was said of him when he died by suicide in 1878, 'Ireland has had enough of him. May she never see his likes again.'

Kitty Kiernan – fiancée of Michael Collins.

Fintan Lalor – his ideas, written in the early nineteenth century, had an influence on the Land League in later years. The inscription on his grave reads: 'we owe no obedience to laws enacted by another country without our consent.'

James Larkin – Irish trade union leader and founder of the Irish Transport & General Workers Union (ITGWU). Known as 'Big Jim' Larkin, he was involved in the 1913 Dublin Lockout.

Joseph Locke – tenor who enjoyed huge popularity in Ireland and England in the middle of the twentieth century. His songs include: 'I'll take you home again, Kathleen' and 'Hear my Song'.

Patricia Lynch – best-selling author of children's books, including The *Turf-cutter's Donkey*. From Cork, she died in 1972.

Seán MacBride – son of Maud Gonne and Major John MacBride, who was executed in 1916. He was founder of Clann na Poblachta and a founder member of Amnesty International. He was awarded the Nobel Peace Prize in 1974.

Edward MacCabe – late nineteenth-century Cardinal Archbishop of Dublin and Primate of Ireland. His impressive tomb/monument occupies a prominent site at the entrance to the cemetery.

James Joseph McCarthy – famous church builder in the nineteenth century.

Muriel Gifford MacDonagh – wife of 1916 leader Thomas MacDonagh and sister of Grace, who married Joseph Mary Plunkett. She died in 1917.

Sean MacEntee – founding member of Fianna Fail and a TD from 1927 to 1969.

Dick McKee – prominent member of the Irish Republican Army during the War of Independence.

Terence Bellew MacManus – Irish rebel and Young Irelander.

Terence MacSwiney – Lord Mayor of Cork who died on hunger strike during War of Independence.

James Patrick Mahon – Irish nationalist politician and mercenary.

James Clarence Mangan – renowned poet and composer of 'My Dark Rosaleen'.

Countess Markievicz – a principled, heroic and enigmatic figure in the Easter Rising of 1916, Constance, Countess Markievicz, was the daughter of Sir Henry Gore-Booth, and married to a Polish aristocrat. After her reprieve from a death sentence for her part in the Rising, she became the first woman to be elected to the UK parliament in 1918. She later became Minister of Labour in the first Dáil.

The Manchester Martyrs – gravestone honouring three members of the Irish Republican Brotherhood (Fenians) known in history as the Manchester Martyrs, who were in fact buried in the grounds of a British prison following their execution after the Fenian Rising of 1867.

Eamon de Valera at Constance Markievicz's funeral. Constance entered hospital in June 1927 and died on 15 July 1927. She was buried in Glasnevin Cemetery in Dublin. (Courtesy of GHS)

British soldiers searching the River Tolka in Dublin for arms and ammunition after the Easter Rising, 1916. (Courtesy of Glasnevin Heritage)

Lance Corporal James Murray – VC recipient (First Boer War).

Dermot Morgan – Irish satirist and star of *Father Ted*. He was cremated in Glasnevin but his ashes are buried in Deans Grange Cemetery.

William Martin Murphy – businessman and one-time owner of Clery's Department Store, the *Irish Independent*, and various hotels and tram companies. He precipitated the infamous and historic Dublin Lockout of 1913.

Patrick Nally – Fenian activist and one of co-founders of the GAA.

James Francis O'Brien – renowned Fenian leader.

Kate Cruise O'Brien – writer and publisher.

William X. O'Brien – politician.

Jimmy O'Dea – celebrated comedian ('Biddy Mulligan, the pride of the Coombe'), actor and Gaiety Theatre pantomime supremo.

Daniel O'Connell – also known as 'the Liberator', he is remembered for his peaceful pursuit of Catholic Emancipation. His grave lies at the right-hand side of the main entrance, marked by a 160ft high tower, fashioned in the style of early Irish Christian monuments.

Daniel O'Connell (6 August 1775–15 May 1847), often referred to as The Liberator or The Emancipator, was an Irish political leader in the first half of the nineteenth century. He was at one time Lord Mayor of Dublin. (Courtesy of GCI)

Eugene O'Curry – nineteenth-century Irish language, history and archaeology scholar.

Patrick O'Donnell – executed in 1883 in London for the assassination of the co-conspirator and turncoat of the Phoenix Park murder, James Carey. A memorial in his honour stands in Glasnevin. He was known as 'the Avenger'.

Patrick Denis O'Donnell – well-known Irish military historian, writer, and former UN peacekeeper.

Jeremiah O'Donovan Rossa – Fenian leader. Patrick Pearse's oration at his funeral in 1915 is celebrated in history. Some of Pearse's words were: 'The fools, the fools, the fools, they have left us our Fenian dead, and while Ireland holds these graves, Ireland unfree shall never be at peace.'

A uniformed Patrick Pearse beside the officiating priest at the funeral of O'Donovan Rossa in Glasnevin Cemetery in 1915. (Courtesy of GHS)

Eoin O'Duffy – Chief of Staff of the Irish Republican Army and leader of the Blueshirts.

Fr Michael O'Flanagan – preacher, Republican and social activist, he died in 1942.

Thomas O'Hagan – 1st Baron O'Hagan and Lord Chancellor of Ireland.

Canon John O'Hanlon – From Stradbally, County Laois, historian and author of the famous *Lives of the Irish Saints*. He died in 1905.

Brian O'Higgins – writer and poet, 1882–1963.

Kevin O'Higgins – assassinated Vice-President of the Executive Council and Minister in the Irish Free State Government.

Mourners at the grave of assassinated Irish Government Minister Kevin O'Higgins in Glasnevin Cemetery, 1927. (Courtesy of UCC Multitext Cultural)

The Governor General of Ireland at the graveside of Kevin O'Higgins, 1927. (UCC Cultural Multit.ext)

Seán T. O'Kelly – Second President of Ireland.

John O'Leary – the Fenian leader celebrated by W.B. Yeats: 'Romantic Ireland's dead and gone; it's with O'Leary in the Grave.' He died in 1907.

John O'Mahony – a founder of the Irish Republican Brotherhood.

Ernie O'Malley – fought in the 1916 Rising and War of Independence. He wrote a number of best-selling books recounting his experiences, including *On Another Man's Wound* and *The Singing Flame.*

James O'Mara – nationalist leader and member of the First Dáil.

Henry O'Neill – painter and archaeologist.

Charles Stewart Parnell – dominant Irish political leader from 1875 to 1891, known to some as 'the uncrowned king of Ireland', he died a year after the scandal of his affair with a married woman (Kitty O'Shea) ruined his political reputation. He was famous for progress in issues of democratic and land reform, including Home Rule and the Land Acts. Though a member of the Church of Ireland, Parnell was buried in Glasnevin in view of its status – at least in the eyes of those who followed him in politics – as the de facto national cemetery. The granite stone that marks his grave was taken from Avondale, County Wicklow, his home for many years.

James Pearse and Margaret Pearse – parents of 1916 Rising leader, Padraig Pearse.

Michael Rahilly – known as 'The O'Rahilly', he was involved in the 1916 Rising.

The grave of Charles Stewart Parnell in 1890s in Glasnevin Cemetery. Behind it, the Round Tower over Daniel O'Connell's tomb can be seen. (Courtesy of GCI)

Parnell's grave, Glasnevin Cemetery, October 1891. Parnell's funeral took place on the 11 October 1891. The vast crowd in attendance, estimated at over 200,000, did not reach the cemetery until dark, and it is said that a meteor was spotted in the sky when the grave was being filled in. One wreath bore the words 'Murdered. Avenge.' This photo was taken on 12 or 13 October 1891. (Courtesy of Kieran Hickey, *The Light of Other Days: Irish Life at the Turn of the Century in the Photographs of Robert French* (1973))

William Rooney – poet and writer who wrote under the pen-name of 'One of the People'. His works invoked the heroes of Ireland's past and were hugely popular in the late nineteenth century.

Patrick (P.J.) Rutledge – Minister in Éamon de Valera's early governments.

Daniel D. Sheehan – first independent Irish labour MP.

Margaret Burke Sheridan – Opera singer who won the admiration of Puccini for her Madame Butterfly. She performed in Covent Garden and La Scala and died in 1958.

Dora Sigerson Shorter – poet and sculptor. Over her grave is an impression working of the Pietá in memory of the 1916 Rising.

George Sigerson – physician, historian and writer.

Francis and Hanna Sheehy Skeffington – the former a pacifist executed in 1916 and his wife, the founder of Irish Women's Franchise League.

Sergeant Philip Smith – VC recipient (Crimean War).

Fr John Spratt – Carmelite priest, founder of the Sick and Indigent Roomkeepers Society, Dublin's oldest charity. He brought St Valentine's body from Rome to Dublin in 1836, where it reposes in Whitefriars Street church.

Austin Stack – patriot and politician who died on hunger strike in 1923.

James Stephens – Fenian leader who died in 1901.

Barry Sullivan – Renowned Shakespearian actor.

Chief Boatswain's Mate John Sullivan – Royal Navy VC recipient (Crimean War).

Patrick James Smyth – journalist and politician.

Matt Talbot – reformed alcoholic much revered by Catholics and called the Venerable Matt Talbot.

David P. Tyndall – prominent Irish businessman who transformed the grocery business.

William Joseph Walsh – Catholic Archbishop of Dublin.

Liam Whelan – an international footballer who played for Manchester United and was killed in the Munich air crash in 1958.

Zozimus – real name Michael Moran, he was a renowned Dublin balladeer and storyteller, known as 'the blind bard of the Liberties'. He died in 1846.

Archbishop Walsh memorial in Glasnevin Cemetery. (Courtesy of GCI)

Funeral procession in April 1921 of Archbishop William Walsh of Dublin, en route to Glasnevin Cemetery. There is a very distinctive memorial to him just inside the gates of the cemetery. (Courtesy of GCI)

James Joyce's life and writing contains many links to Glasnevin Cemetery, the heart of the Hibernian necropolis. Glasnevin played a pivotal role through out the life, time and imagination of Joyce: from the Hades Chapter in *Ulysses*, which is set in the cemetery, to the Joyce family grave which is the final resting place of his parents.

Glasnevin Cemetery also contains war combatants and range from those who fought with Wellington in the Napoleonic campaigns, through to the American Civil War, the trenches of the First World War and the Irish Civil War. Sometimes these men and women returned to a hero's welcome, but more often than not, they returned to a life of obscurity and an unmarked grave. Here you will find soldiers from the Royal Engineers and Irish Guardsmen buried near Irish Volunteers.

MONUMENTS TO THE GREAT

There is a huge variety of monuments and memorials in the cemetery represent an interesting collection of Irish designs, including carved shamrocks, Irish wolfhounds, harps, and high crosses. The original wooded paths have been retained, and there are mature native trees, plus imported species such as Cedar of Lebanon and Giant California Sequoia.

People in the nineteenth century were very concerned with how they would be portrayed in death, and their families and friends also used funerals and monuments to proclaim their own political or social status. Consequently, the cemetery displays some fine examples of the work of some of Ireland's greatest sculptors, stonemasons and architects, including John James McCarthy, James Pearse (father of 1916 Rising leaders, Padraig and Willie), John Hogan and Thomas Farrell.

High crosses abound in the cemetery, with every form of interlaced ornament and carved scenes. Ireland's original garden cemetery is also home to some exquisite examples of classical, gothic and Celtic architecture, and within its grounds are buried many of the artists who shaped modern Irish art. Some of the graves of notable people from the arts world over the past 180 years include Thomas Farrell, Albert Power, J.J. McCarthy and Leo Whelan and some former members of the RHA.

George Coppinger Ashlin designed the enormous monument/mausoleum to Cardinal McCabe, who died in 1885. It is cruciform in shape with a mosaic floor and symbols of the four Evangelists, while the figure of the cardinal is guarded by angels. It is a very striking example of craftsmanship. The Sir John Gray Monument commemorates his good works (including the provision of the Vartry water supply scheme), on behalf of the people of Dublin.

In contrast to the Gray and McCabe monuments, the work and achievements of Charles Stewart Parnell are not celebrated in his gravestone, which is a massive granite boulder simply inscribed 'Parnell'.

Other fine nineteenth-century sculptors whose work is represented in the cemetery include Sir Thomas Farrell, John Hogan, Christopher Moore, John Thomas Papworth and George Coppinger Ashlin.

Archbishop McCabe
monument,
Glasnevin Cemetery.
(Courtesy of GCI/GCM)

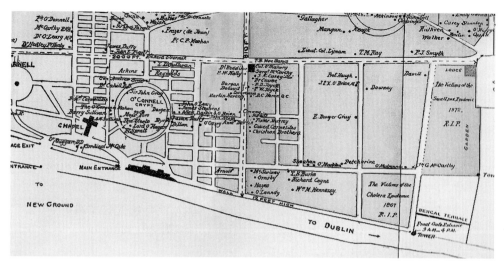

Late nineteenth-century map of Glasnevin Cemetery, showing prominent and important burial sites. (Courtesy of GCI)

CEMETERY PLOTS

Bodies were interred in a variety of places, ranging from the most expensive vaults to the cheapest plots in the common ground where, in the nineteenth century, multiple burials took place. Graves were marked and recorded using a grid system. The first designated poor ground area opened in June 1839, the site of which is now west of the Finglas Road entrance gates.

Many religious orders own plots in the cemetery, including the Dominicans, the Franciscans of Merchants Quay, the Carmelites of Whitefriar Street and the Jesuits, in whose plot are interred the remains of the poet Gerard Manley Hopkins.

There is an Irish Army plot, while members of the army who are killed serving with the United Nations are buried in the UN plot. A Republican plot contains the remains of those involved in both the War of Independence and the Civil War.

The Collins/de Valera divide lives on in the graveyard and Michael Collins' grave is eternally adorned with fresh flowers. All played an influential role in the introduction of so many social reforms and of the rights and privileges that we enjoy today.

Glasnevin is, and has always been, a multi-denominational cemetery. Buried and cremated here are Catholic and Protestant, Sikhs and Jews,

Flowers at Michael Collins' graveside, Glasnevin, 1922. (UCC Cultural Multitext)

Inside Glasnevin Cemetery, *c.* 1900. (Courtesy of Robert French/GCI)

Members of the Four Courts Garrison visiting the Republican Plot in Glasnevin Cemetery in 1953. (Courtesy of the Irish Volunteers Commemorative Society)

Visiting Michael Collins' grave in 1939. (Courtesy of Glasnevin Heritage)

rich and poor. The cemetery is home to the Millennium Plot (what would have formerly been known as a 'paupers plot'). This is looked after by the charity 'Alone', founded by Dublin fireman, Willie Bermingham, who maintain the plot and make sure people buried there are buried with dignity, giving them a full funeral, headstone and flowers. In one of the older paupers' plots, up to 25,000 bodies are buried in a relatively tiny area, not far from Parnell's grave. Many of the dead were victims of a cholera outbreak in the late nineteenth century. A couple of years after their burial, fresh outbreaks of cholera were reported in the Drumcondra/ Ballybough area. For not far beneath the soil where their bodies lay is a maze of underground streams, all emptying into the Tolka River – the disease had assimilated into the soil and on into the water, making its way back into circulation.

THE O'CONNELL MEMORIAL

The crypt of Daniel O'Connell has been recently refurbished and is open to visitors. Former Irish President, Mary McAleese, who officially reopened the monument, described O'Connell as not just a major figure in Irish history, but also in British and world politics.

He died in Genoa, while on a pilgrimage to Rome. He requested that his heart be taken to Rome and the rest of his body to Ireland. O'Connell's coffin has been entombed since 1869 by a large altar stone of black Kilkenny marble with the Durrow Cross inscribed into it. Ten members of O'Connell's family are also laid to rest in the crypt. The coffin may be seen and touched through a number of portals cut into the stone.

A tower above the crypt is one of Dublin's landmarks, standing 168ft tall and dominates the entrance to the cemetery. The idea originated with renowned antiquarian George Petrie. He was very interested in ecclesiastical architecture and especially old monastic ruins and round towers. He originally intended a group of buildings – the round tower, a Celtic cross and a chapel similar to Cormac's Chapel in Cashel, County Tipperary. The Cemetery Committee were impressed with his ideas and work began. However, the huge expense incurred on the tower meant that the remainder of the project was abandoned.

Daniel O'Connell (6 August 1775–15 May 1847). (Courtesy of GCI)

Early twentieth-century view of the Round Tower over Daniel O'Connell's tomb. (Courtesy of GCI)

O'Connell's remains were finally placed in the crypt beneath the tower in 1869, having been in a nearby vault before that.

Visitors to the cemetery will be able to climb the tower for the first time in nearly forty years from 2014. The internal steps were unfortunately destroyed by a bomb in 1971, attributed to Loyalists in retaliation for the blowing up of Nelson's Pillar on Dublin's O'Connell Street on 8 March 1966. The new winding wooden steps will bring visitors to the top of the monument where there will be a viewing platform. According to the Glasnevin Trust, 'with Glasnevin on an elevated site, some 110 feet above sea level, the new facility will provide visitors with spectacular views from four windows – from the Mourne Mountains to Wicklow and to Ireland's Eye.'

CURRAN AND PROSPECT SQUARES

The oldest part of the cemetery is called Curran's Square and is near the original entrance gate at Prospect Square. It is named after John Philpot Curran, patriot, lawyer and parliamentarian, and father of Sarah Curran, the beloved of Robert Emmet. Other sections include the Garden Section, St Brigid's Garden, St Patrick's and the O'Connell Circle Section. This latter section contains vaults approached by descending steps. This was the most expensive area in which to be buried and only coffins made of lead were allowed.

In the late 1870s it was decided to build a new entrance gate, situated on the Finglas Road, to cater for the expanding needs of the cemetery. The old entrance was somewhat awkward to access, and was remote from the O'Connell Memorial, which the Cemetery Committee wished the public to see on entering the cemetery. Also, it was felt that a new entrance would divert the funeral crowds from the pub situated beside the old entrance! The committee also made the decision, for this reason, to have funerals before noon.

Once opened, the new entrance became the most fashionable place to be buried and there are many fine monuments in this area. Important figures in politics and the Church were buried near the new gates.

Whilst amongst the masses of graves, friends and comrades lay side by side, mortal enemies are often not within a short distance of each other either. For while Big Jim Larkin turns to dust beneath the Glasnevin soil, likewise does William Martin Murphy, whose palatial tomb is within sight of the modest grave Jim Larkin and his family are buried in. While Frank Ryan is buried within sight of the gate, so too is General Eoin O'Duffy of the Blueshirts; both are veterans, on different sides, of the rise of Fascism in Europe in the 1930s.

THE ANGELS PLOT AND THE SQUINTING WINDOWS

In earlier times, stillborn babies were not allowed in blessed ground, as they were not baptised. Many babies were therefore buried in the ditches and hedges on the outside of cemeteries around the country. Often parents buried their babies themselves between dusk and dawn, in fear of being caught and yet wanting their baby to buried in holy ground. However, the old Angels plot at Glasnevin Cemetery was one of only a few places that allowed stillborn

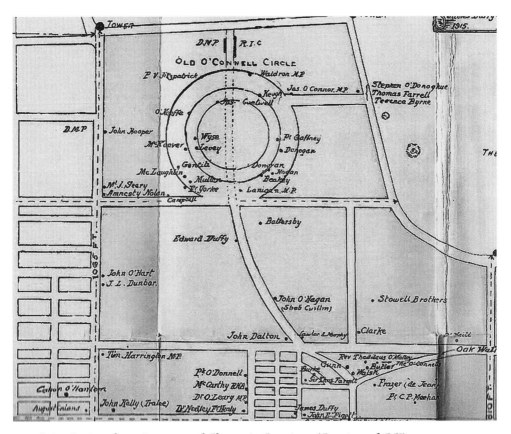

Late nineteenth-century map of Glasnevin Cemetery. (Courtesy of GCI)

children to be buried on consecrated ground. The little angels plot is the final resting place to over 50,000 infants who were buried there up to the 1970s.

Glasnevin is also the last resting place for the remains of Ireland's forgotten and unwanted; the group known as the Magdalene Women, those unfortunate women who committed no other crime than to fall foul of the 'squinting windows' mentality and society's fear of unmarried women and their children.

INDIAN MUTINEERS

There is also an interesting memorial to the Indian Mutineers of 1920. Upon hearing of the War of Independence in their homeland, hundreds of Irish soldiers fighting in the British Army in India turned their guns on their generals. Though close to 400 men took part, the mutiny was quickly suppressed and eighty-eight of those men were court martialled. Fourteen were sentenced to death and the rest given up to fifteen years in jails in Dagshai and Solan. Two died in the mutiny, Private Sears and Private Smyth. Thirteen of the men sentenced to die had their sentences commuted to life imprisonment, though one man, James Daly, was shot dead by firing squad. He was considered the leader of the mutiny at just 21 years old.

ZOZIMUS

Glasnevin Cemetery is also the last resting place of the renowned Dublin balladeer Zozimus, or Michael Moran as he was originally known, a blind storyteller who lived in Fumbally Lane in the heart of Dublin's Liberties during the nineteenth century. He was also known as the 'Blind Bard of the Liberties' and the 'Last of the Glee Men'. He was born about 1794 off Blackpitts/Fumbally Lane, in Faddle Alley. A fortnight after his birth he became blind from illness, and consequently became a blessing to his parents (such were the times), who were soon able to send him to rhyme and beg at street corners and at the bridges over the River Liffey. He developed an astounding memory for verse and he made his living reciting poems, many of which he had composed himself, in his own lively, though semi-literate, manner. By the time he had grown to manhood, he was the admitted king of all the ballad-mongers of the Liberties. Zozimus combined the great ability to memorise old poems, songs and stories with an incredible flair for composing and reciting his own.

Moran's nickname derived from a poem written by Bishop Anthony Coyle of Raphoe about St Mary of Egypt. According to the legend, she had followed pilgrims to Jerusalem with the intent of seducing them, then, turning penitent on finding herself prevented from entering the church of the Holy Sepulchre by a supernatural force, she fled to the desert and spent the remainder of her life in solitary penance. When she was at the point of death, God sent Zozimus of Palestine to hear her confession and give her Holy Communion, and a lion to dig her grave. The poem was so popular when recited by the blind balladeer, and so often called for, that Moran was soon nicknamed 'Zozimus'.

In his last few years, his voice grew weak and was costing him his only means of livelihood. He ended up feeble and bedridden and he died on 3 April 1846 at his lodgings in 15 Patrick Street, aged around 61, and was buried in Glasnevin Cemetery. He had feared grave-robbers ,who were rife in Dublin at the time.

His grave remained unmarked until the late 1960s, when the famous traditional Irish ballad group, the Dublin City Ramblers, erected a tombstone in his memory. The grave is still intact in the Poor Ground of the cemetery and can be located not far from Daniel O'Connell's burial site.

His epitaph reads:

My burying place is of no concern to me,
In the O'Connell circle let it be,
As to my funeral, all pomp is vain,
Illustrious people does prefer it plain.

WAKING THE DEAD:
THE BATTLE OF GLASNEVIN GRAVEYARD

From 1791, bodies of the executed were dissected for medical research. As the number of medical schools increased and demand exceeded supply, medical students, or their agents, resorted to stealing newly-interred bodies. The agents were known as 'resurrectionists' or 'sack-'em-ups'. What greatly

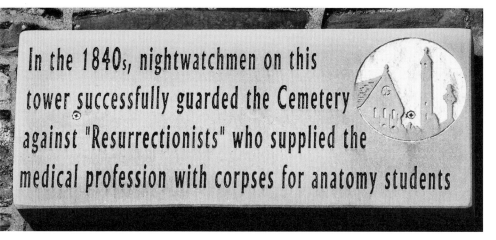

In the 1840s, nightwatchmen on this tower successfully guarded the Cemetery against "Resurrectionists" who supplied the medical profession with corpses for anatomy students

Wall plaque on original watchtower near the entrance to Glasnevin Cemetery. The cemetery is surrounded on all sides by high stone walls, with towers on each corner. Not there to keep the dead in, they were built to keep grave-robbers out. Grave robbing was a lucrative business in the nineteenth century, with corpses fetching £2 each, quite a sum in those days. Guards manned the towers from dusk to dawn, armed with muskets and pistols. (Courtesy of Glasnevin Trust/GCI)

facilitated this macabre business is that there was no law against the stealing of dead bodies. Dublin folklore is full of stories about the body snatchers and grave-robbers linked to Glasnevin. And there is much truth in the stories. Zozimus wrote a poem showing his fear of the 'sack-'em-ups' in which he begged his long-established companion, 'Stony Pockets', to save him from the 'Sack-'em-ups':

Oh Stony, Stony
Don't let the Sack-'em-Ups get me
Send round the hat
And buy me a grave.

Grave robbing could often end in violence as gangs of (usually armed) grave robbers clashed with trigger-happy (and possibly drunk) watchmen and the police. This was the reality portrayed in Dr John Fleetwood's book, *The Irish Body Snatchers*. Fleetwood extensively quotes from *Saunders' Newsletter*. Published between 1746 and 1879, it's a wealth of contemporary information relating to 'sack-'em-ups' and resurrection men: a subject which never seemed to have failed to sell newspapers.

One of the most amazing incidents chronicled in *Saunders' Newsletter* is the 'Battle of Glasnevin Graveyard' which took place in January 1830.

The remains of the late Edward Barret Esq., having been interred in Glasnevin churchyard on the 27th of last month, persons were appointed to remain in the churchyard all night to protect the corpse from the 'Sack-'em-Up gentlemen', and it seems the precaution was not unnecessary, for, on Saturday night last, some of the gentry made their appearance, but soon decamped on finding they were likely to be opposed.

Nothing daunted however, they returned on Tuesday morning with augmented forces, and well armed. About ten minutes after two o'clock, three or four of them were observed standing on the wall of the churchyard, while several others were endeavouring to get on it also. The party in the churchyard warned them off, and were replied to by a discharge from firearms. This brought on a general engagement; the Sack-'em-Up gentlemen fired from behind the tombstones. Upwards of 58 to 60 shots were fired, one of the body snatchers was seen to fall; his body was carried off by his companions. Some of them are supposed to have been severely wounded, as a great quantity of blood was observed outside the churchyard wall, not withstanding the ground was covered with snow.

And, just when things were looking pretty grim for the enterprising body snatchers, they got a bit grimmer.

During the firing, which continued for upwards of a quarter of an hour, the church bell was rung by one of the watchmen, which with the discharge from the firearms, collected several of the townspeople and the police to the spot – several of the former, notwithstanding the severity of the weather, in nearly a state of nakedness; but the assailants were by this time defeated and effected their retreat. Several headstones bear evident marks of the conflict, being struck with balls etc.

However, the body snatchers returned the following night:

On Sunday night or early Monday morning a party of persons who are familiarly called the sack-'em-Ups visited Glasnevin Churchyard. An armed party was watching a corpse that had been deposited there during the day and observing those humble friends of science and humanity getting over the wall they fired on them. Some of them must have been wounded as blood was afterwards discovered on the wall. The same party stationed themselves in the churchyard the following evening when they discharged a few shots to let the resurrectionists know they were at their posts.

Glasnevin Cemetery still bears the scars and effects of the time; the watchtowers of the ever-vigilant guards are still visible today.

GLASNEVIN CEMETERY TODAY

Glasnevin Cemetery remains under the care of the Dublin Cemeteries Committee. The development of the cemetery is an ongoing task, with major expansion and refurbishment work being carried out at the present time. The cemetery museum is well worth a visit. An interesting notice on the pedestrian gate beside the old entrance at Prospect Square states: 'Photography is permitted ... but please respect the privacy of those interred here'.

Mass is celebrated by members of the parish clergy every Sunday at 9.45 a.m. The annual blessing of the graves takes place each summer, as it has done since the foundation of the cemetery in 1832. The best way to visit the cemetery is to take one of the daily tours which will bring to life the rich and important stories of those buried here.

4

THE CHURCHES –
ST MOBHI'S,
'THE WOODENER',
ST COLUMBA'S

In 1618, Glasnevin became part of the parish of Clontarf. In 1879 this parish was divided by Archbishop McCabe, and Glasnevin and Ballymun became part of Fairview Parish. In 1881, the Wooden Church was built at Glasnevin as a chapel of ease to Fairview. In 1912, the Parish of Glasnevin was created.

ST MOBHI'S CHURCH

St Mobhi's church (Church of Ireland) is the oldest 'in use' structure in Glasnevin, at nearly 800 years old. The church's history can be traced back to 1240 and it is believed to have been built on the site of an even older chapel, possibly part of St Mobhí's monastery. That monastery existed between *c.* AD 530 and 900. The year 900 coincides roughly with the attacks of Ireland's east coast by the Vikings and Danes. The Vikings established settlements and trading ports. The Danes, however, attacked the east coast for whatever they could plunder. In their flat-bottomed boats, the invaders would have had access to Glasnevin's hinterland via the Tolka River, thus making the monastery easy prey for them. The Danes were expelled from Ireland in 1014, after the famous Battle of Clontarf, and the Vikings eventually assimilated into the population.

Outside St Mobhi's church, Glasnevin, 1971. (Courtesy of Nannson/ Dublinforums.net)

Early twentieth-century image of Old Churchyard beside St Mobhi's church, Church Avenue. (Courtesy of St Mobhi's church)

St Mobhi's church, Glasnevin. (Courtesy of Nannson/Dublinforums.net/St Mobhi's church)

To the Glory of Almighty God
for Victory granted in the Great War of 1914 to 1918
the people of Glasnevin Church have caused this monument to be erected
in token of their gratitude to Him
and in proud remembrance of the bravery and devotion
of those their fellow worshippers whose names it bears,
and who gave their lives for the honour and safety of their country,
and to secure the freedom and the welfare of their fellow men

CHARLES FREDRICK BALL, 7™ R.D.F.
FRANCIS BOXWELL, H.M.S. "GOOD HOPE."
THOMAS HENRY DIXON, 4™ R.D.F.
CHARLES DOUGLAS HILL, 6™ K.L.R.
SAMUEL STEUART KENNEDY, 4™ R.D.F.
GEORGE WALTER THOMAS LINDSAY, R.F.A. & R.F.C.
CLAUD FREDERIC THOMAS LINDSAY R.F.A.
ARCHIBALD THURSTAN THOMAS LINDSAY, R.E.
RICHARD DAMER MANLY, R.I.R.
SIDNEY FREDERICK MILLER, R.A.S.C.
EDWARD FRANK RUTLEDGE, 1ˢᵗ R.I.R.
HARRY CECIL SPRUCE, R.A.S.C.

Irish First World War Memorial in St Mobhi's church, Glasnevin. (Courtesy of St Mobhi's church/Michael Pegum)

The Vikings mostly used timber for their buildings, and the church here was constructed employing methods later introduced by the Normans. Improvements and extensions were added in the seventeenth and nineteenth centuries. Sir John Rogerson, who owned Glasnevin House, was particularly instrumental in renovating the old church in the early 1700s. The church has a small and atmospheric ancient cemetery in its grounds – probably the original Glasnevin Cemetery.

THE WOODENER, THE WIGWAM AND THE PYRAMID – OUR LADY OF DOLOURS' CHURCH

Towards the end of the nineteenth century, the Archdiocese of Dublin decided that the growing population of Glasnevin needed a church. In 1881, a site of the banks of the River Tolka was purchased and a wooden church erected there. This church had been built in two months! The timber church, which originally stood on Berkeley Road, was moved to the riverside site (overlooking the Botanic Gardens) on Botanic Avenue. The altar in this church was from the

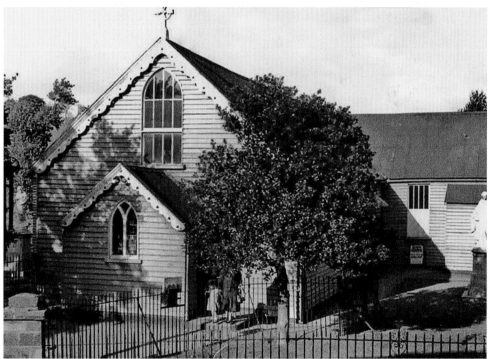

The Wooden Church (Our Lady of Dolours), 1950s. The church was demolished in 1963. (Courtesy of Damntheweather/Dublinforums.net)

Construction of the new Our Lady
of Dolours' church, 1963.
Formerly known as the Wooden
Church or Woodener, the new church
is known locally as the Wigwam
(or Pyramid) church due to its shape.
(Courtesy of GCI)

Our Lady of Dolours' church,
Glasnevin. (Courtesy of
Damntheweather/Dublinforums.net/
Our Lady of Dolours' church)

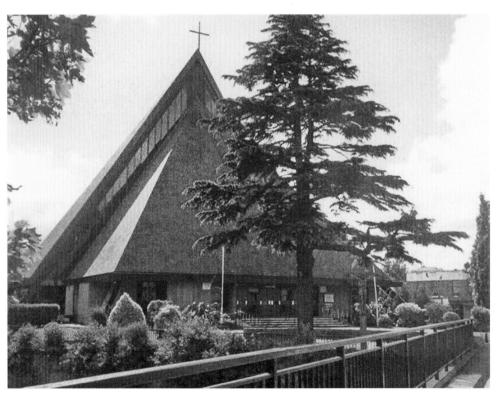

notorious Newgate Prison in central Dublin. In 1912, when Glasnevin officially became a parish, the wooden structure served as the parish church until it was replaced, in 1972, by then new Our Lady of Dolours' church. This building has a very distinctive pyramidal appearance, particularly when viewed from Botanic Avenue. The old church was known locally as 'The Woodener' or 'The Wooden' and the new building is still known to older residents as 'The New Woodener' or 'The Wigwam'.

A view of Our Lady of Dolours' church, Glasnevin from the National Botanic Gardens. (Courtesy of Nansson/Dublinforums.net and Our Lady of Dolours' church)

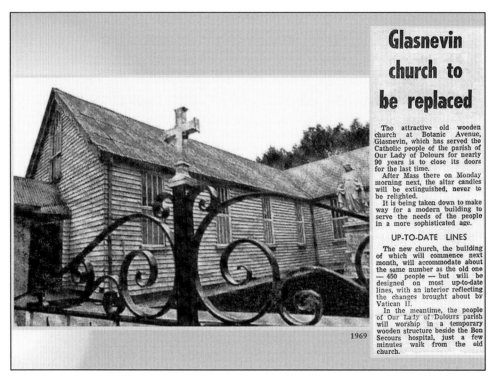

The 'Old Woodener' church on Botanic Avenue, 1969. (Courtesy of Glasnevin Heritage)

ST COLUMBA'S AND THE PENNY HOUSE

Meanwhile, in 1902, plans for another church were being mooted in Glasnevin – that of St Columba's on Iona Road – to cater for the growing population resulting from the construction of new houses. However, since there was no church, the locals had to share the Wooden Church, which by then had been extended and refurbished.

Acquiring a site for a new Catholic church, in a district where most of the land lay in the hands of Protestants, led Fr John Byrne to the Redemptoristine Sisters in St Alphonsus Convent in Drumcondra, who sold him a 6-acre section of their farmland for £1,200. Work started on the site in 1903 and the foundation stone was laid and blessed on 7 August, three days after the election of Pope Pius X, giving St Columba's the honour of being the first church in Christendom to have his name engraved on its cornerstone.

Designed by Dublin architects Ashlin and Coleman, it took two years to complete and cost a total of £24,000. The official opening and blessing took place on 15 October 1905, with the appointment of Fr John Byrne as parish priest.

The church was dedicated to St Columba because of his Glasnevin connection. This can be traced back to St Mobhi's sixth-century monastery on Glasnevin Hill, where Columba was said to have studied before embarking on his journey to the Scottish island of Iona, where he established a similar monastery.

The church itself owes much to the Celtic Revival in style that was very much in vogue in Ireland at the turn of the twentieth century. The baptismal font, the stations of the cross, and, in particular, the original pulpit with carved figures, are noteworthy.

Across the road from the church is No. 94 Iona Road, a detached home overlooking the grounds of Iona church. It was known as the 'Penny House' because it was raffled by the Church in 1905, with tickets costing a penny. Fêtes and bazaars were important forms of fundraising for religious and charitable events during the early twentieth century. A fundraising

On 22 January 1958, hotelier Carl Opperman married Florence Towey, the eldest daughter of the Towey family from Ballinisland, Foxford, County Mayo. They married at St Columba's church, Iona Road, Glasnevin, Dublin. (Courtesy of Opperman family/GCI/ St Columba's church)

leaflet from the time is highly decorated and is a good example of the Celtic iconography popular at the time. It reflects the Celtic Revival that had such a major influence of subsequent Irish history – particularly the 1916 Rising. The leaflet also shows how the Rotunda in Dublin's city centre continued to be used as a location for major fundraising events two centuries after its foundation, especially those of a charitable nature.

The parish hall or centre, Claude Hall on Claude Road, was originally the home of the Ancient Order of Hibernians and was purchased by the parish in 1928. For many years it housed the Glasnevin branch of the Catholic Young Men's Society (CYMS), an organisation that was at the forefront of the Catholic Action Movement in Ireland, particularly from the 1920s until the 1950s. Their particular concerns were directed against the threat of Communism. The organisation had a huge influence in shaping the moral ethos of Ireland in the first half of the twentieth century.

The hall itself was a very active social centre for the parish and was highly regarded as a venue for dances and concerts. Over the years, many other parish and residential groups used the hall.

St Columba's church organist, Maureen Valentine, and the Iona Ladies Club and various other clubs are fondly remembered. Interestingly, one of Maureen Valentine's students is the renowned Irish composer and member of Aosdana (academy of creative artists), Michael Holohan, who has won numerous awards for his compositions and had his music performed at home and abroad.

Despite being near the church, access to the hall from the direction of the church is by a pedestrian bridge over one of the two railway lines that run through Glasnevin. After many years and lots of happy memories for the people and parish of Glasnevin, the hall was sold in 2003 to facilitate the refurbishment of St Columba's church and the building of a new parish centre.

5

SCHOOLS
AND SPORT

THE INKBOTTLE AND THE MODEL

At the top of Botanic Avenue, near the present-day Our Lady of Dolours' church, a school was erected by Dr Delaney in 1715. Jonathan Swift, a friend of Delaney's, is said to have suggested the design to Delaney. Over the years it became a landmark known as 'The Inkbottle' because of its unusual circular structure with a conical roof, resembling an ink bottle. It was demolished in 1901 and a new school was built on the site that still stands.

Nearby, and just beside St Mobhi's church, is the old Model School. The building remains, but towards the end of the nineteenth century changed from the model school idea back to a regular school. Today it is used as an Educate Together school. From 1845, model schools were established for the training of young teachers and were overseen by inspectors from the National Education Board. The Glasnevin Model School on Church Avenue was built in 1847. As well as the 3Rs, children were taught needlework, agriculture and horticulture.

Glasnevin Model School pupils after making their Confirmation, 1926. (Courtesy of Glasnevin Heritage)

First Communion of boys from Glasnevin National School, 1960s. (Courtesy of Glasnevin Heritage/John Moore)

Young Glasnevin children in the early 1960s. (Courtesy of Glasnevin Heritage)

Other important schools in the area include Lindsay Road National School, a Presbyterian school opened in 1911 on Lindsay Road. One of Dublin's oldest Gaelscoil, where all the subjects are taught in Irish, is Scoil Chaitriona, which opened in 1928. Due to increased demand, it moved to new premises on Mobhi Road in 1972. It has since gone from strength to strength.

ST VINCENT'S CBS

In 1856, the Society of St Vincent De Paul (the Vincentians, not the charity) purchased a building in Mount Brown, near Kilmainham, to cater for boys who had lost their parents. Within a year, this building proved to be too small, so land was purchased at the junction of Finglas Road and Botanic Road and a very imposing building was erected behind the railings where the apartments in Dalcassian Downs now stand. This had accommodation for 150 boys and also provided school facilities. It was known as St Vincent De Paul Orphanage but the boys were always called boarders. There was also a farm attached, which provided most of the milk and vegetables needed. By the time of its centenary in 1956, very little had changed as there were still 140 boarders and the farm was still in operation.

Pupils at St Vincent's School, Glasnevin, 1958. (Courtesy of Glasnevin Heritage)

Boys sitting outside St Vincent's School, Glasnevin, in the early twentieth century. (Courtesy of the Vincentians)

Meanwhile, the running of the school changed hands. In 1863, the Congregation of Christian Brothers took over from the Congregation of the Holy Ghost (Spiritans). Day boys were enrolled from January 1927, but this put a strain on the accommodation and a new primary school building was opened in 1939, St Vincent's CBS Primary School. The secondary school continued to operate in the old building until new buildings were opened in 1964. Boarding continued until 1973, when the school became entirely a day school. The swimming pool was built in 1968 and the sports hall followed in 1976. The main school frontage is now on Finglas Road, opposite the historic Glasnevin Cemetery.

FAMOUS FACES

Some famous past pupils include:

In sport: Paul Caffrey, Gaelic football; Senator Éamon Coughlan, Olympic and World Champion Athlete; Kenny Cunningham, soccer; Dessie Farrell, Gaelic football, hockey and CEO (Gaelic Players Association); John Furlong OC OBC, CEO (Vancouver Whitecaps FC, 2010 Olympic and Paralympic Winter Games); Pat Hickey, president of the Olympic Council of Ireland; Gerry McCaul, former Dublin Senior football manager; Mick and Con Martin, soccer; Jason Sherlock, Gaelic football; and Harry Thuillier, Olympic fencer and broadcaster.

In arts and media: Patrick Collins HRHA, painter; Ronan Collins, RTÉ broadcaster; Patrick Cosgrave, journalist and writer; Jack Cruise, theatre actor and comedian; Vincent Doyle, journalist and editor of the *Evening Herald* and the *Irish Independent*; Aidan Gillen, stage and screen actor; Aidan Leonard, RTÉ broadcaster and 2fm director of music; Pat Liddy, artist, historian, author and environmental lobbyist; Frank McDonald, environment editor of *The Irish Times*; and Paul Reynolds, RTÉ crime correspondent.

In politics and diplomacy: Sean Alyward, Secretary of the Department of Justice; Fr John Fogarty CSSp, Superior General, Congregation of the Holy Spirit (Spiritans/Holy Ghost Fathers); H.E. Declan Kelly, ambassador; Dr John O'Connell, politician (TD, Ceann Comhairle, Senator and MEP); and Francis Martin O'Donnell, senior UN official and ambassador.

ST MARY'S HOLY FAITH SECONDARY SCHOOL

The Holy Faith Sisters have contributed enormously to the field of education in Glasnevin for over 100 years. The story of the present St Brigid's School (on the Old Finglas Road) began in 1863, when the Sacred Heart Sisters purchased Sir John Rogerson's large country residence in Glasnevin, then known as Glasnevin House. Using this building, the Sacred Heart sisters opened the first Catholic 'poor school'.

In 1865 Margaret Aylward, foundress of the Holy Faith Sisters, acquired Glasnevin House (formerly the home of Revd Charles Lindsay) from the Sacred Heart Sisters and took over the school. Margaret Aylward, along

Miss P.Dalton, Mrs Henry, Sr. Consilio, Mrs. Deneher, Miss Cox, Mrs.O'Reilly,
Mr. Hallinan, Miss Nolan, Mrs Ryan, Mr. McGill; Mr. Cullen, Miss Jansson,
Miss Hallinan, Sr. Mary, Miss Leahy, Miss O'Brien, Miss Mullen, Mrs Ryder,
Miss Hynes, Ms. McCauley, Miss McCarthy, Mr. Nolan; Miss Mullens, Miss Corr,
Miss Kavanagh, Miss Murphy, Miss Aird, Sr. Assumpta, Mrs. Forde, Mrs. Moran,
Mr. Kearney, Miss Walker, Miss O'Mahoney; Sr. Conleth, Mrs Doyle, Mrs Flynn,
Fr. Jack, Sr. Maria Monica, Mr. Cummins, Miss Curran, Miss Rooney, Sr. Helen

Staff from the Holy Faith Secondary School in the early 1970s. (Courtesy of Glasnevin Heritage)

with fifteen other Holy Faith sisters, extended the school and added a fine
new school building, now known as Aylward House. She renamed the
school St Brigid's, just like all of the other Holy Faith primary schools that
she went on to establish. This school served as St Brigid's Primary School in
Glasnevin for the next 100 years.

Margaret Aylward also founded St Mary's Secondary School, in 1873.
The present secondary school was opened in 1941, under the direction of
the Holy Faith sisters. The school is in the grounds of the Holy Faith Convent,
which borders the Botanic Gardens, Glasnevin Cemetery and St Brigid's
Primary School. In the 1920s, St Columba's Primary School was opened by
the Holy Faith sisters.

SPORTING LIFE

Glasnevin is home to a variety of sports clubs. Soccer is played by local clubs
Tolka Rovers, Glasnevin FC and Glasnaion FC, basketball is organised by

Clonliffe Harriers team photograph 1908/09, taken outside the Prospect Square old entrance gate to Glasnevin Cemetery, and just beside the 'Gravediggers' (Kavanagh's) Pub. (Courtesy of GCI)

Tolka Rovers and tennis is played in Charleville Lawn Tennis Club. The tennis club was founded in 1894 by a small group of tennis enthusiasts, headed by a Mrs McConnell. Charleville took its name from the original location at the corner of the Charleville and Cabra Roads and the move to its present location on Whitworth Road took place in 1904. The club boasts a membership of 400 senior and junior members and the club has won many Dublin Lawn Tennis Council titles, above the average for a club of their size.

Hockey is played at the Botanic Hockey club on the Old Finglas Road while Glasnevin Boxing Club and Football (soccer) Club has a clubhouse on Mobhi Road.

Scouting has a strong tradition in Glasnevin, with 1st Dublin (LHO) Scout Troop located on the corner of Griffith Avenue Extension and Ballygall Road East. The scout group celebrated its 100 years of scouting in 2011, making it one of the longest-established scout groups in the world.

NA FIANNA GAA CLUB

The Gaelic games of football, hurling, camogie and handball are all organised locally by Na Fianna CLG. It promotes Gaelic games and the traditional Irish pursuits of music and dance. Céilí music and dancing is a regular feature in the club hall, while informal music sessions are held in the members' bar.

Na Fianna was officially formed as a club on 25 April 1955, when 201 members transferred from C.J. Kickham GAA Club to form Cumann Luthchleas Gael Na Fianna. The first Annual General Meeting took place on 27 October 1955. Na Fianna's first clubhouse was originally transported from the Guinness Sports Grounds in Crumlin to Mobhi Road but was burnt to the ground in May 1967.

Being in the parish of Glasnevin, Na Fianna connects to the many families resident in the Mobhi Road/ Homefarm Road/ Ballymun Road/ Botanic Road axis, while extending its influence to the edges of Phibsboro, North Circular Road, Glasnevin Avenue, Drumcondra Road and Griffith Avenue, thus taking in all the Iona and Drumcondra residents too. The club also has affiliations with the many schools, both primary and post-primary, in this wide catchment area. The liaison between the club and schools offers parents and children a consistent engagement in sporting and non-sporting activities.

Na Fianna has been a leading proponent of Irish culture, and the Na Fianna Céilí has long been a tradition of the club. The club's involvement in GAA Scór is an extension of its own regular internal Scór sessions. Na Fianna has won the Dublin Senior Football Championship on five occasions, first in 1969 and the second time exactly ten years later. They eventually began their famous championship treble exactly twenty years later, in 1999 and completing the treble in 2001.

Na Fianna's dominant sport is football, but hurling, camogie and handball are also played.

Na Fianna Senior Ladies team won the County Championship in 2009, the first time the ladies section have won a championship at senior level. The score was 1–11 Na Fianna, 1–10 Naomh Marnog. The senior ladies won their second title against Ballyboden St Enda's in July 2011. In 2008, Na Fianna's u14 football team won the first of three consecutive Feile Peile na nOg Division One All-Ireland titles.

Young Glasnevin hurlers, 1962. (Courtesy of Irish Press/Glasnevin Heritage)

Notable players associated with the club include: Joey Boland, current Dublin inter-county hurling player; Tomás Brady, current Dublin inter-county football player; John Caffrey, former Dublin inter-county football player; Paul Caffrey, former Dublin inter-county manager; Senan Connell, former Dublin inter-county football player and TV3 pundit; Dessie Farrell, former football player and current GPA chief executive; David Graves, former Dublin inter-county hurler; Kieran McGeeney, former Armagh inter-county football player and former Kildare inter-county football manager; Enda McNulty, current Armagh inter-county football player; and Jason Sherlock, former Dublin inter-county football player.

6

MUSIC
AND DRAMA

THE GLASNEVIN MUSICAL SOCIETY

One of Dublin's most famous musical societies has to be the Glasnevin Musical Society. Founded in 1958 by the late Fr O'Brien, the society has embodied the spirit of that first show, *The Desert Song* with the renowned John Hanson of BBC fame, all through the years since.

The society has come a long way since its beginnings in Glasnevin's Wooden Church. The society has been ambitious and professional from the start and consequently has grown from strength to strength and has consolidated its place as one of the most dynamic amateur organisations in the Irish music scene, through the high standard of its productions. In 1959, the society performed *The Student Prince* to great acclaim. It soon outgrew the St Francis Xavier Hall and in 1960 moved to the classical surrounds of the Olympia Theatre, opening with a performance of *The Lily of Killarney*.

During its first decade, it staged a number of musicals and operettas, from the wispy heather of the fictitious *Brigadoon* to the glamour of *Die Fledermaus*.

The 1970s was an important decade in the life of the society. In 1972, it made its first appearance in the Gaiety Theatre with a production of *The Merry Widow*, an operetta which has remained a redoubtable favourite with the society and audience alike. In 1976, it embarked on the immensely popular *Favourite Melodies* series, and also had a new addition to the society with the esteemed Music Director, Colman Pearce, who took control of the baton; a role he holds to this day. The society ended the 1970s celebrating its 21st birthday with a *Gala Concert* in the RDS and, of course, *The Merry Widow*.

The 1980s marked the return of operettas (*Die Fledermaus* and *The Irish Ring*), together with numerous concerts. In 1984, the society held the unique honour of being the first group to present a fully staged and choreographed show in the National Concert Hall with a production of *The Gypsy Baron*.

In the 1990s, the society was invited to partake in the hugely successful production of *Me and My Girl* in the Olympia Theatre. The Chorus has been invited on many occasions to perform with renowned artists and has guested for RTÉ productions, many of which have been broadcast on both television and radio. A true highlight, however, was the society's invitation to sing with Perry Como in his *Perry Como's Irish Christmas Show*, recorded at the Point Theatre in 1993. This show was televised worldwide and has been broadcast coast to coast on American television every Christmas since. In 1998, the society was honoured to perform for the President of Ireland, Mary McAleese, at a family day in Áras an Úachtaráin.

The society began the new millennium with a modern mix to its repertoire, the very successful *Showstoppers* series, which has grown from year to year. A choreographed and costumed energetic production, *Showstoppers* combines favourites from Broadway and the West End to the silver screen. The society was also fortunate to be invited to perform at the very memorable Opening Ceremony of the Special Olympic Games in Croke Park in 2003. No decade would be complete without the favourite *The Merry Widow*, and the society enjoyed a sell-out show in the National Concert Hall in 2005. It also marked another special anniversary – thirty years of the *Favourite Melodies* series, which was celebrated with a fantastic concert in 2006.

Recent years have seen the society as busy as ever and the staging of new shows to add to the society's repertoire, with *Chess* in 2007 and *Jekyll & Hyde* in October 2008, both in the National Concert Hall.

According to a recent review in the *Sunday Business Post*:

> ... a show that will be remembered as one of the finest musical productions ever staged at the National Concert Hall. The challenge now facing the Glasnevin Musical Society is that, having scaled new heights with [*Jekyll and Hyde*], it will have to work its socks off to stay there. But it will be worth it.

It all began with incredible excitement back in 1958, and as the society looks to the future, it can still capture that excitement of opening night and has brought much enjoyment, happiness and laughter to audiences throughout the decades of its success. The show must go on and today, rehearsals continue in Dublin City University and the Glasnevin Lawn Tennis Club.

The year 2005 was a special year for the Glasnevin Musical Society as it presented an operetta that was a hugely popular part of their wide repertoire. Moreover, it was a special year for *The Merry Widow* itself as it was the centenary of the first performance of this magical operetta in Vienna in December 1905. When introduced to London, Dublin, New York and elsewhere, it was a huge success. Indeed, such was the response to it that a craze in New York for Merry Widow hats, shoes and even Merry Widow cigars and chocolates, developed, and became must-have accessories. Merry Widow cafés sprang up overnight and ladies took to wearing Merry Widow corsets!

The Glasnevin Musical Society over the years developed a special place for *The Merry Widow* in the hearts and minds of members and fans of the Society. First presented by the Society in 1972 in Dublin's Gaiety Theatre, the show was revived in 1979 due to popular demand. The phenomenal success of *The Merry Widow* continued in the 1980s and 1990s with sell out shows in the National Concert Hall. It was therefore a fitting tribute that the Society presented the operetta, again in the National Concert Hall in 2005, the perfect birthday gift to this venerable 'Queen of Operettas'. Furthermore, the opening night was on St Valentine's Day! One of Ireland's finest sopranos, Virginia Kerr, was the leading lady of the show in one of her favourite roles as Anna Glavari in this wonderful production. And of course it has a very popular storyline all about deception, romance, a country in need of its people, and naturally a 'happy ever after' finale!

THE LINDSAY SINGERS AND THE IONA PLAYERS

The Lindsay Singers, the Iona Drama Group and the Iona Players are just some of the other stage groups that played and continue to play a prominent role in the life and story of Glasnevin. The Claude Hall Players were active in the 1940s and '50s, particularly with their annual pantomime. In the 1970s, the Iona Players (originally called the St Columba's Drama Group) were formed; one of their first productions was *Troubled Bachelors*. Success followed with *Sive* and other productions. One of their most successful and memorable was *Ritual for Dolls*. The Abbey Theatre's Thomas McAnna described it a 'pure theatrical magic and wonderfully entertaining'.

The Lindsay Singers, also hailing from Glasnevin, are nationally-famous in Ireland, often appearing on RTÉ, and in the National Concert Hall, such is their talent. The choir was founded in 1958 by Ethna Barror from Lindsay Road. Her family background was music. Over the years the choir won many awards and accolades and appeared in many festivals. *The Irish Times* reported on a performance in the RDS in 1973 and noted, 'one's admiration for Mrs Barror's training remains at a peak.'

Regarded as one of the most significant and successful choral conductors in the country, Ethna Barror was invited to become Honorary Life President of the Association of Irish Choirs in 1993. Her contribution to choral singing in the country stemmed not only from her inspirational work with the Lindsay Singers since 1958, but with the countless other school and community choirs and musical societies with which she worked. Having had notable successes in performance, Mrs Barror was also in regular demand as an adjudicator.

> It seems remarkable that there was ever a time without them [The Lindsay Singers], so firmly has she implanted them in our hearts and so strikingly high a standard has she brought them to from just about the beginning. Every choir thinks that it aims for perfection: hardly any achieve it, but then Mrs Barror is unique. (Charles Acton, *Irish Times*, May 1984)

In the late 1990s, the choir was voted 'Choir of the Year'. In 2001, the Lord Mayor of Dublin presented them with the Vocal Heritage Award for their contribution to music in Ireland over the years. After a long lifetime filled with such achievements, Ethna Barror died in 2011, in her 96th year.

THE ABBEY AND THE ALLGOODS

The Glasnevin Youth Concert Band is also a musical group of some renown, not only in Glasnevin, but in the wider country, having performed at many venues over the years.

Two renowned Abbey actresses, Sara and Molly Allgood, were from Claude Road. Molly played many roles, including Pegeen in Synge's *The Playboy of the Western World*. Another Abbey Theatre stalwart was Eileen

Crowe from Carlingford Road, while theatre critic Gabriel Fallon hailed from around the corner at Whitworth Road.

Given all that talent in the area, it is not surprising that Glasnevin is also home to The Helix arts centre, which includes Ireland's largest theatre, the Mahony Hall.

7

ROADS AND PUBS – STELLA, STRAIN AND THE GRAVEDIGGERS

Old Dublin bridge to be rebuilt

Irish Press reporter

GLASNEVIN bridge over the river Tolka, is to be rebuilt by Dublin Corporation at a cost of £60,000. Work on the project began yesterday morning and it is expected that it will take at least eight months to complete.

Traffic will be diverted via St. Mobhi Road and St. Mobhi Drive while the work is in progress, but arrangements for pedestrian traffic over the river will be made.

The bridge, which is between 100 and 150 years old, has three arches and buttresses in the river, but the new bridge will be a single-span job which will give freer passage to the river and will reduce somewhat the risk of flooding in the area.

Wider

The roadway and footpaths are 39 feet wide from wall to wall at present, while the new bridge will be some 50 feet wide. It will be a rigid, portal frame type and will be cast on the site.

The corners into St. Mobhi Drive and Botanic Avenue will be eased while the work is in progress.

1967 article in the *Irish Press* on Glasnevin Bridge over the River Tolka. The sketch (inset) depicts the old tri-arched bridge. The sketch, by Brendan Scally, was made in 1952. (Courtesy of Glasnevin Heritage)

There was a time, 200 years ago, when there were turnpike gates on the main roads at each side of Glasnevin. Daniel O'Connell eased the burden on those travelling to the newly opened Prospect Cemetery by opening up another road, Prospect Avenue, through the heart of Glasnevin. Turnpikes were eventually abolished in 1855.

In the 1930s, with the expansion of Glasnevin, the Dublin Corporation decided to call the main new road Dean Swift Road. However, Canon Dudley, parish priest of the Wooden Church nearby, objected. He was successful and the road was named Mobhi Road instead. However, the Corporation did not forget their hopes, and the bridge over the Tolka at the beginning of Mobhi Road was named Dean Swift Bridge. Furthermore when Glasnevin North developed in the 1940s, a small road linking Mobhi Road to Rathlin Road was called Stella Avenue after his lifelong companion. In the Wadelai Estate, Swift is also remembered with names such as Dean Swift Road, Delville Road and Drapier Road.

A PLACE OF GRANDEUR AND DIGNITY

There are many fine roads in Glasnevin: Botanic Road and Avenue, Lindsay Road, Delville Road, Crawford Avenue, Fairfield Road, Claude Road,

Cliftonville Road, Iona Road, Gartan Road, St Mobhi's Road and Avenue, Marguerite Road, St Canice's Road, St Columba's Road, Prospect Road, Glasnevin Hill, Mobhi Road and Avenue and the surrounding areas, etc. Botanic Avenue was originally called Corry's Lane after a James Corry, linen merchant. Prospect Square and DeCourcey Square are hidden enclaves in the heart of old Glasnevin. More recent housing developments include Dalcassian Downs, Glasnevin Downs and Glasnevin Wood, as well as Glasnevin North.

Colm Graham grew up in Glasnevin. He recalls the area from his childhood:

There is something very elegant and refined about (Glasnevin parish). Young families were growing up in the newly-constructed homes that were mushrooming in the early nineteen hundreds. There was an element of nobility in the design of those red-bricked houses with the signature block of the builders, Strain and Boyd, on the façade of each, and well-trimmed flowering front gardens added further grace and liveliness to make (a place) of grandeur and dignity.

IONA ROAD

Iona Road is one of the most sought-after residential roads on the north side of Dublin and it has long been regarded as one of the most prestigious locations in Glasnevin. The roads adjacent also share this accolade. This is partly thanks to the Lindsay family, who stipulated in 1902, when selling 9 acres of land to the Catholic Church for the building of St Columba's church, that six houses of 'good quality' had to be built as part of the agreement. This led to the opening of Iona Road, initially called Crawford Road after the Lindsays. (Adjacent roads to the church were also to be called after the Lindsays – Crawford Avenue, Claude Road and Lindsay Road.) Iona Road began as a series of short terraces entered from Botanic Road with open fields nearby. The early occupiers of these fine houses would have been the new young Irish men and women, who would have been the first generation of Catholics to have received secondary and third-level education. A new confidence was emerging. Upstanding stockbrokers, teachers and solid middle-class families bought these new houses.

Houses of Iona Road, one of the most sought-after residential roads on the north side of Dublin. This handsome Alexander Strain-built semi-detached residence captures all the charm and elegance associated with the Edwardian era. (Courtesy of Myhome.ie/GCI)

At the height of the Celtic Tiger boom, properties on Iona Road were asking upwards of €900,000. The handsome Alexander Strain-built residences capture all the charm and elegance associated with the Edwardian era. Most of the redbrick houses still have all the original features one would expect, including marble fireplaces, timber floors, ornate ceiling covings and plasterwork and picture rails. The accommodation in a typical Iona Road family home today comprises a large entrance hall with beautiful stained glass, panelled hall door, and curved plasterwork on the ceiling. A large drawing room with high ceiling, featuring an impressive marble or slate fireplace with tiled inset, the bay window flooding the sitting/drawing room with light and double doors leading to the dining room/ family room, also with original marble fireplace and detailed plasterwork. Steps lead down to a family dining area, or breakfast room and kitchen, utility room and WC. Upstairs there are between three and five bedrooms, some with cast-iron fireplaces, with the main room spanning the width of the house with an en suite shower room.

Strain used granite cornerstones and granite edging beneath each bay window. A point of interest is that most of these homes are unique in some detail, having agreed such an arrangement with the vendor, Henry Gore Lindsay, though all were built to similar measurements to give a visual harmony to the road. When one walks or drives up Iona or Lindsay Roads, one's attention is drawn to this harmony, reinforced by the continuous and dominant redbrick appearance. The spectacle is particularly enhanced by each house having the stained-glass panelling on the front door.

PLACES AND FACES

Some famous former residents of Iona include Emmet Dalton, the Irish Free State officer and companion to General Michael Collins on the day of his assassination, who lived near St Columba's church and later on Iona Road. Cecil Barror, the well-known and popular Radio Éireann actor and presenter, lived opposite the Maples Guesthouse. His wife, Ethna Barror, was equally famous and was the founder and director of the acclaimed 'Lindsay Singers'. Jimmy Campbell, the famous Theatre Royal conductor and presenter, lived further along Iona Road.

James Joyce, author of *Ulysses* and other famous works has connections with Glasnevin. Not only is the famous cemetery included in his work, but his father spent his final years lodging with a Church of Ireland family, the Medcalfs at 25 Claude Road. He died in December 1932, and the funeral took place in nearby St Columba's church, followed by interment in Glasnevin Cemetery. James Joyce's relations, the Murrays, had family in the area too – Charles J. Murray, a solicitor, was a cousin. The house, on the corner of St Columba and Iona Roads, is often regarded as the setting for Joyce's *Finnegan's Wake.*

Botanic Avenue was the home of Brendan Bracken, who became an advisor to Winston Churchill during the Second World War. Madge Adcock, a daughter of local developer, Alex Strain (who started building houses on Lindsay Avenue in the early years of the twentieth century) lived on Hampstead Avenue. She was one of the founders in 1955 of St Michael's House for disabled children. T.R. Harrington, editor of the *Irish Independent*, lived on Iona Park. Irish War of Independence hero, Ernie O'Malley (*On Another Man's Wound*

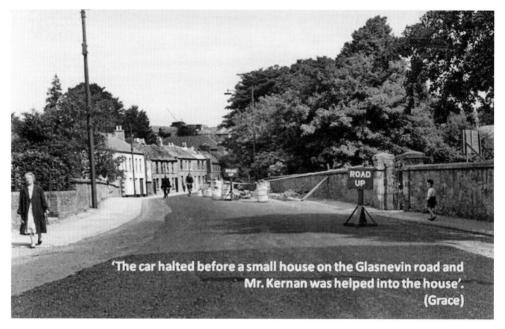

'The car halted before a small house on the Glasnevin road and Mr. Kernan was helped into the house'. (Grace)

Glasnevin in the 1960s. The quote is taken from James Joyce's *Ulysses*. (Courtesy of Glasnevin Heritage)

and *The Singing Flame*) was born in County Mayo and later his family moved to Dublin and Iona Drive. A compatriot of his, Dan Breen (*My Fight for Irish Freedom*), recounts an experience he had in Glasnevin. He was on the top deck of a tram when he noticed two Black and Tans sitting near him. He stood up, and just as he was drawing his gun, the Tans jumped over the sides of the tram in fear of their lives!

Former Lord Mayor of Dublin in 1907 and 1908, J.P. Nanetti, lived on St Patrick's Road. Prominent public servant Tom Barrington, founder of *Administration* and the Institute of Public Administration, lived on Iona Crescent. The former director of the Central Statistics Office was Roy Geary of St Brigid's Road.

BOTANIC ROAD

Botanic Road is at the heart of Glasnevin. It was along this route, opposite the entrance to the gardens, that the old village was situated. This part of the road and the adjacent Prospect Road have the old rural atmosphere with different house structures – some big, some cottages. The entrance to the gardens is marked by two similarly built old ivy-clad houses standing guard, one each side of the old turnstile and main gates.

One of the landmark buildings along this road is the Smurfit Printing Works that was formerly the John Player Cigarette Factory. The factory was located here as land in the 1920s in the area was quite inexpensive. Messrs Players set up their cigarette factory in the Carroll Estate and employees were housed on Hollybank Road (management) and Botanic Avenue (general staff). Alex Thom, the famous printers of *Thom's Street Directory* for Dublin, was also located on the estate. Across the road from the industrial estate is the fine building dating from 1913 that is the Botanic House pub and restaurant.

Botanic Avenue links Glasnevin with Drumcondra and a one-time local name for it was 'Slut's Alley'. The two areas join at the steps to Mannix Hill. The oldest properties include those in Addison Place and the former shop premises (Tino's) opposite the church car park. The dispensary was built at the turn of the twentieth century, as were the redbrick house and the adjoining roads. Amongst them is a detached single-storey dwelling thought to date from the mid-1800s. Some of the attractive houses on the road were built for the employees of the newly opened Player's Cigarette Factory.

A great view of the Player's Tobacco Factory taken from the roof of No. 67 Botanic Road in the mid-1930s. Notice the tram lines on the road. (Courtesy of Glasnevin Heritage)

HART'S CORNER

Approaching Glasnevin via Phibsboro is what is now known as Hart's Corner but which about 200 years ago was called Glasmanogue, and was then a well-known stage on the way to Finglas. At an earlier date, the name possessed a wider signification and was applied to a considerable portion of the adjoining district. The lovely circle that is Hart's buildings was completed in 1925.

GRIFFITH AVENUE

Griffith Avenue runs through Glasnevin, Drumcondra and Marino. The avenue spans three electoral constituencies, and is the longest tree-lined avenue in the Northern Hemisphere with no retail outlets. It was named after Arthur Griffith, who was the founder and third leader of Sinn Féin and also served as President of Dáil Éireann. Arthur Griffith was buried in Glasnevin Cemetery.

Griffith Park playground, near Iona Road, 1965. (Courtesy of Nannson/Dubilnforums.net)

Striking image of Corpus Christi Church on Griffith Avenue. (Courtesy of Nansson/ Dublinforums.net and Corpus Christi Church)

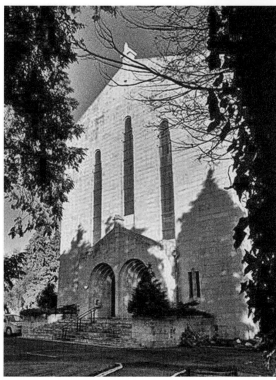

Front of Corpus Christi Church on Griffith Avenue. (Courtesy of Nansson/Dublinforums.net and Corpus Christi Church, Griffith Avenue)

GLASNEVIN HILL AND MET ÉIREANN

In 1975 the new headquarters of Met Éireann, the Irish Meteorological Office, opened just off Glasnevin Hill, on the former site of Marlborough House. Like the nearby Catholic church, the Met Éireann building was built in a somewhat pyramidal shape by Sisks and designed by Liam McCormic. It is recognised as one of the most significant, smaller commercial buildings, to be erected in Dublin in the 1970s. Met Éireann is the leading provider of weather information and related services for Ireland. The 'Winking Weatherman' was for many years one of its most popular personalities on the RTÉ nightly weather report.

The headquarters of Met Éireann, the Irish Meteorological Service, Glasnevin Hill. (Courtesy of Met Éireann/GCI)

TRAMS AND TRAINS

With the expansion of the Drumcondra, Clonliffe and Glasnevin Township in the closing decades of the nineteenth century, the promoters of tramways in Dublin saw new opportunities and the North Dublin Street Tramways' Company was set up to take advantage of the growing population in these burgeoning areas. In 1875, the company laid down three lines to service these areas. Soon horse-drawn trams were ferrying residents into the city from Tolka Bridge. From the bridge up to the terminus at the Holy Faith Convent, a third horse was harnessed to bring the tram up the steep hill. The trams operated every twenty minutes.

In 1899, the electric tram was introduced and the line was extended over the bridge in 1903. The founders of the Township admitted that the opening of the tramway gave a huge boost to the areas. In 1939, trams were replaced by buses and in later years, the old cobblestones and tram lines were removed.

The No. 19 tram plied its way along Botanic Road to and from the city. This service was later augmented with the No. 14 that crossed the city from

Irish Volunteers marching along Prospect Road, near Cross Guns Bridge, to Glasnevin Cemetery in 1915, for the funeral of Jeremiah O'Donovan Rossa. (Courtesy of Irish Volunteers Commemorative Committee)

Dartry to Finglas Road. The trams were open-topped with a spiral staircase at each end. It cost one penny to travel from Iona or Botanic Road to Nelson's Pillar in O'Connell Street.

The start of the twentieth century saw the opening of a short-lived railway station on the Drumcondra and North Dublin Link Railway line from Glasnevin Junction to Connolly Station (then Amiens Street): it opened in 1906 and closed at the end of 1907. Glasnevin railway station opened on 1 April 1901 and closed on 1 December 1910. The Midland and Great Western Railway also passed through the area parallel to the Royal Canal and Whitworth Road, with stops near the Dublin Flour Mills at Cross Guns Bridge. The old flour mills are still standing, having been converted into apartments in recent years. They were a hive of activity for years, with horse-drawn barges along the canal making and collecting cargo.

PUBS OF GLASNEVIN – BRIAN BORU, THE WASHERWOMAN AND THE GRAVEDIGGER

Glasnevin is blessed to have some of Dublin's most famous pubs located within its boundaries. The Sunnybank Inn, Addison Lodge, the Botanic

The Washerwoman's Hill Restaurant, Glasnevin Hill. The building dates from 1700 and is one of the oldest buildings in the village. The restaurant was re-opened in 1996. The name derives from the old washhouse (laundry) that was situated on the hill. (Courtesy of Washerwoman's Hill Restaurant)

House, the Washerwoman's Hill Restaurant, Hedigan's the Brian Boru and Kavanagh's the Gravediggers are all long-established and renowned public houses.

JOHN KAVANAGH'S PUB – THE GRAVEDIGGERS

Kavanagh's Pub, hidden in Prospect Square in the heart of Glasnevin, is also known as 'The Gravediggers' because of its proximity to Glasnevin Cemetery – beside Prospect Gate. The gravediggers of old would pop in for a pint after a hard day's work, and one such story goes that coffins were seen outside the pub while the workers went for a quick drink! The pub was also known over the years as 'The Deadman's Pub'.

The current proprietor is Eugene Kavanagh and his family have owned the pub since 1833. The interior has changed little since the nineteenth century. The pub featured in a television advertisement for Smithwick's beer.

John Kavanagh's 'Gravediggers' Pub in Prospect Square, Glasnevin. (Courtesy of John Kavanagh's/GCI)

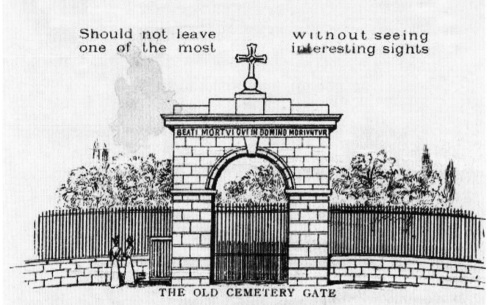

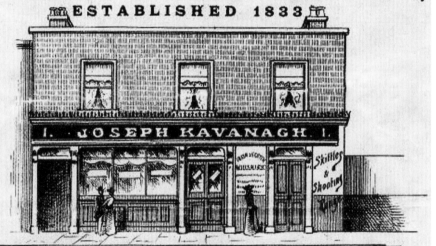

Late nineteenth-century poster from Kavanagh's 'Gravediggers' Pub. It features the old entrance gate to Glasnevin Cemetery. (Courtesy of Kavanagh's Pub)

Charles Stewart Parnell's family at Glasnevin Cemetery, October 1891. Pictured the day after Parnell had been interred are his sister, Mrs Emily Dickinson; his brother, Henry Tudor Parnell, and one of his nieces, Alfreda or Delia McDermott. (Courtesy of GHS)

Steeped in history, the Gravediggers is a pub that encourages a little reflection and a lot of conversation. It feels a little like stepping back in time, and is definitely worth stopping at if you are visiting the area.

HEDIGAN'S – THE BRIAN BORU

On entering Glasnevin via the Cross Guns Bridge, one of the first buildings on your left is the famous pub that commemorates Brian Boru. There has been a public house on the site of Hedigan's, The Brian Boru', for over 200 years. However, the association of Brian Boru – High King of Ireland – goes back 1,000 years, as it was here that his army camped prior to his victorious Battle of Clontarf, fought on Good Friday 1014. The present building dates from the 1850s, with the façade virtually unaltered since then. The pub has a large painting just over the entrance with a depiction of Brian Boru on his horse, leading his army into battle, and carrying a crucifix over his head – hence the claim that it is the only pub in Ireland with a cross outside it!

In 1904, Patrick Hedigan, a native of Galbally, County Limerick purchased the Brian Boru. The pub has long been something of a landmark, and very atmospheric inside, with old pictures of Dublin adorning the walls. It is famous as a venue for meals and refreshment following funerals in the nearby Glasnevin Cemetery. Indeed, the Brian Boru is mentioned in *Ulysses* as Joyce's party of mourners pass by on their way to Glasnevin Cemetery.

The pub was also renowned for its special 'Powers White Label' whiskey which Patrick Hedigan bonded and blended to his own recipe and served from the wood. The renowned Glasnevin-born poet, Oliver St John Gogarty, born in 1878 (son of local property owner Dr Gogarty of Fairfield House), recalled in later years that from an early age he regarded this establishment, which he passed daily, as having the finest pub front in Ireland!

THE BOTANIC HOUSE

It is quite easy to pass this pub and not appreciate what a fine redbrick and impressive building it is. The best vantage point is across the road, so that one can look at it from a distance. Opened in 1913, under the ownership of Mrs Temple, it had a grocery store and a retail wine and spirit bar on the ground floor, with a large window to display goods, it had extensive accommodation on the upper floors, including five bedrooms, drawing and dining rooms and servants' quarters. When completed, it was regarded as one of the largest and most handsome business establishments in the area.

ANDERSON'S FOOD HALL/BUTCHERS

Although this long-established Glasnevin business in not a pub, it is fondly remembered in Glasnevin. Andersons Continental Style Cafés was started by Noel Delany and Patricia van der Velde in 2003, with the opening of Andersons Food Hall and Café on The Rise in Glasnevin, just off Griffith

Avenue. Noel's father originally operated Anderson Smith Butcher's from the same premises for over fifty years. The premises, built in the 1930s, underwent a major design and refit in 2003, but retains many of the existing fine architectural features, including the façade and the original tiled floor from the butcher's shop, giving it the atmosphere of a 'bouchon'; a butcher-cum-restaurant typical of the French city of Lyon.

Other pubs include the Sunnybank Inn (famous for decades for its Cabaret), the Washerwoman's Hill in one of the oldest buildings in Glasnevin, the Addison Lodge, and the Tolka House.

Gents' hairdresser, Prospect Avenue, Glasnevin, 1970. (Courtesy of Glasnevin Heritage)

Merville Dairy, Glasnevin in late 1950s. (Courtesy of Glasnevin Heritage)

Protesting in 1971 outside Marlborough House at the appalling living conditions of the residents. Marlborough House in Glasnevin, Dublin was registered as a detention centre for up to fifty boys and operated from 1944 to 1972.

The former Iona Garage near Cross Guns Bridge, Glasnevin, in the early twentieth century. Note the cobblestones and the tram tracks. (Courtesy of Glasnevin Heritage)

Whelan's Newsagent, Botantic Road, 1973. (Courtesy of Glasnevin Heritage)

FURTHER READING

F.E. Ball, *A History of the County Dublin* (1920)

Ray Bateson, *Dead and Buried in Dublin* (2002)

Douglas Bennett, *Encyclopaedia of Dublin* (1991)

Centenary Committee of St Columba's Church, Iona Road, *Heart of Iona – A People, A Parish, A Place* (2005)

Carmel Connell, *Glasnevin Cemetery, Dublin 1832–1900* (2004)

Dillon Cosgrove, *The Tolka, Glasnevin and the Naul Road from North Dublin* (1909)

Maurice Curtis, *The Liberties* (2013)

Maurice Curtis, *Rathmines* (2011)

John D'Alton, *A History of the County Dublin* (1838)

Mary Daly, *Dublin: The Deposed Capital* (1984)

Mary Daly, Mona Hearn, Peter Pearson, *Dublin's Victorian Houses* (1998)

Nicholas Donnelly, *Short History of Dublin Parishes: St Columba, Drumcondra. Part XIV* (1915)

Dublin Cemeteries Committee, *Glasnevin Cemetery: An Historic Walk* (1997)

Duchas Heritage Service, *The Botanic Gardens* (n.d.)

M.J. Egan, *The Story of Glasnevin* (1961)

M.J. Egan, *The Parish of St Columba* (1961)

William Fitzpatrick, *Catholic Cemeteries* (1900)

John Fleetwood, *The Irish Body Snatchers* (1988)

Weston St John Joyce, *The Neighbourhood of Dublin: Glasnevin, Finglas and the Adjacent District* (Third and enlarged edition, 1920)

Samuel Lewis, *A Topographical Dictionary of Ireland* (1837)

Teresa Murphy (ed.), *Heart of Iona: A People, A Parish, A Place. Celebrating 100 Years of St Columba's Church 1905–2005* (2005)

E. Charles Nelson & Eileen McCracken, *The Brightest Jewel. A History of the National Botanic Gardens, Glasnevin, Ireland* (1987)

Tony O'Doherty, *A History of Glasnevin, Its Village, Lands and People* (2001)

R.J. O'Duffy, *Historic Graves in Glasnevin Cemetery* (1915)

Seamas O'Maitiu, *Dublin's Suburban Town 1834–1930* (2003)

If you enjoyed this book, you may also be interested in...

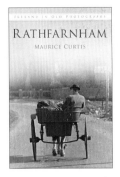

Rathfarnham In Old Photographs
MAURICE CURTIS

Rathfarnham one of the most fascinating and attractive parts of South County Dublin. Over the years it has witnessed some of the pivotal events in Irish history and has been home to some of the most important people in Irish social, religious, political and economic history; people who have left us a lasting legacy in the areas of culture, sport, music, art and literature. In this illustrated history, Maurice Curtis has created a vibrant and valuable record for all those with an interest in the life and times of Rathfarnham.

978 1 84588 825 1

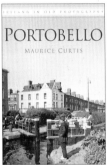

Portobello In Old Photographs
MAURICE CURTIS

In this book, Maurice Curtis takes the reader on a visual tour of Portobello through the decades, recounting both the familiar and the events and places that have faded over time, revealing many fascinating details, including the fact that Dublin's Portobello was named after an area on the East Coast of Panama! This, and much more, is captured in a timeless volume, which pays fitting tribute to this well-loved part of the city.

978 1 84588 737 7

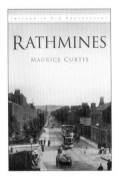

Rathmines In Old Photographs
MAURICE CURTIS

Rathmines is one of the country's best known suburbs, home to heads of government, vast swathes of students and local families alike. In his latest book, writer and historian Maurice Curtis takes the reader on a visual tour of Rathmines through the decades, recounting both the familiar and the forgotten, those features and events that may have faded over time. Illustrated with over 150 archive photographs, this fascinating book pays fitting tribute to the place Rathmines has carved in the history of all who have passed through it.

978 1 84588 704 9

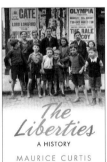

The Liberties
MAURICE CURTIS

Following the murder of Thomas á Becket, King Henry II decreed that an abbey be founded close to the present-day St Catherine's church, Thomas Street, Dublin, in Becket's memory, and the monks that founded it were to be free from city taxes and rates. This 'Liberty' expanded and took in the part of Dublin which today is known as the Liberties, one of Dublin's oldest and most interesting parts. In this book, author Maurice Curtis explores this fascinating history and its significance to the people of Dublin.

978 1 84588 771 1

Visit our websites and discover thousands of other History Press books.

www.thehistorypress.ie www.thehistorypress.co.uk